"In this book, Mark does a fantastic job of moving from theory to practice. He uncovers the angst that lies beneath much of what we call youth ministry and helps us transform that fear into loving attention to God and young people. A master storyteller, Mark is able to show how a youth ministry based upon 'practicing the presence of God' is not so much about technique, but about how we as adults live our lives in relation to ourselves, our God, and our youth."

- DANIEL WOLPERT, AUTHOR OF *CREATING A LIFE WITH GOD* AND *MEETING GOD IN VIRTUAL REALITY*

"Mark Yaconelli dispels the myth of youth running around in monk robes, burning incense, and chanting hymns (even though I think that would be interesting to see) and opens up the real world of contemplative youth ministry being all of life in relationship to God, our creator. This book speaks volumes about what we really need to be attending to: Our relationships with God, our relationships with ourselves, and our relationships with the youth we have been called into ministry to serve."

- SUSAN H. HAY, DIRECTOR, MINISTRIES WITH YOUTH, GENERAL BOARD OF DISCIPLESHIP

"If you read only one book on youth ministry this year, *Contemplative Youth Ministry* is the one you should choose. If you're yearning for 'something more' in your faith, this is a powerful challenge to really come alive. Mark Yaconelli writes out of his breadth and depth of experience with young people and with spiritual deepening. Through anecdotes and stories from his own ministry, Mark invites us to radically rethink both why and how we do youth ministry."

- CHRIS DOUGLAS, DIRECTOR OF YOUTH/YOUNG ADULT MINISTRY, CHURCH OF THE BRETHREN GENERAL BOARD

"The approach to ministry that Mark Yaconelli offers in this book has been absolutely transformational for my ministry and my life. This simple approach to ministry comes down to an equation: Love God and love each other. If we do that in our ministries, we will find that the programs and big events and rules for keeping the church carpet clean will all take care of themselves. If we love, we will find that there is room for the Holy Spirit to move among us, and even share in the spiritual practice of 'contemplative karaoke.' Enjoy the journey!"

- REV. WALLACE R. SMITH, FIRST BAPTIST CHURCH OF INDIANAPOLIS, YOUTH MINISTRY RESOURCE TEAM, AMERICAN BAPTIST CHURCHES, USA

"*Contemplative Youth Ministry* is not only a book filled with practical direction, but also it comforts and encourages the soul. You will identify with Mark Yaconelli's life if you've spent any length of time ministering to students. I was moved to tears as Mark shared his struggles with the unrealistic pressure and humiliation that we often feel in youth ministry."

- MARK MATLOCK, AUTHOR, SPEAKER, AND PRESIDENT/FOUNDER OF WISDOMWORKS MINISTRIES

# CONTEMPLATIVE YOUTH MINISTRY

## PRACTICING THE PRESENCE OF JESUS

**Mark Yaconelli**

Foreword by Anne Lamott

ZONDERVAN™

GRAND RAPIDS, MICHIGAN 49530 USA

ZONDERVAN.COM/
AUTHORTRACKER

**Youth Specialties**

www.youthspecialties.com

*Contemplative Youth Ministry: Practicing the Presence of Jesus*
Copyright © 2006 by Mark Yaconelli

Youth Specialties products, 300 South Pierce Street, El Cajon, CA 92020 are published by Zondervan, 5300
Patterson Avenue Southeast, Grand Rapids, MI 49530.

**Library of Congress Cataloging-in-Publication Data**

Yaconelli, Mark.
  Contemplative youth ministry : practicing the presence of Jesus / by Mark Yaconelli.
    p. cm.
  ISBN-10: 0-310-26777-3
  ISBN-13: 978- 0-310-26777-5
  1.  Church work with youth. 2.  Contemplation. I. Title.
  BV4447.Y23 2006
  259'.23--dc22

                                                                                    2005037968

The Scripture quotations contained herein are from the New Revised Standard Version of the Bible, copy-
righted 1989 by the Division of Christian Education of the National Council of Churches of Christ in the
United States of America, and are used by permission.

Web site addresses listed in this book were current at the time of publication. Please contact Youth Specialties via e-mail (YS@YouthSpecialties.com) to report URLs that are no longer operational and replacement
URLs if available.

*Creative team: Doug Davidson, Randy Southern, Heather Haggerty, Laura Gross, and Mark Novelli*
*Cover design by Burnkit*
*Printed in the United States*

06  07  08  09  10  •  10  9  8  7  6  5  4  3

# Dedication

For Jill,

Your love continues to be my deepest experience of God's grace.

and

For Dad

Your passion for life still burns within me.

This is the first, wildest, and wisest thing I know: that the soul exists, and that it is built entirely out of attentiveness.

—MARY OLIVER

# Contents

# Foreword

Several years ago, the Christian Education team at Saint Andrew Sunday school found itself floundering. We had been holding classes for children during the regular worship service for years, and while we all felt called to teach our young ones, it was hard. We'd figured out a few basic concepts—i.e., children loved to hear Bible stories, loved to talk about them as the stories related to their own lives, and especially loved the arts and crafts projects that illustrated that day's message. We had marvelous curriculum, and we had stacks and stacks of juice boxes.

But there was something missing.

It was sometimes so hard to keep their precious attention. It was hard to impart our love of God to them while letting them be children—with a great deal more physical energy (and needs) than us and with their own eyes through which they were seeing this increasingly scary world.

We read books and consulted a few experts and talked to the children and grew in Jesus, and still we floundered. Our classes usually felt like us-against-them situations, exactly what you don't want in a church school. But we were the big people—we made the rules, led the class in prayer, doled out the snacks, attempted to maintain discipline, and tried as well as we could to share the experience, strength, and hope we had found in Christ. And they were small and fast and fidgety, frequently annoying, and wanted to talk about themselves. They sometimes misbehaved and took each other's food and pushed and shoved and all spoke at once. *Ahhh!*

We tried everything, especially prayer. But on bad days the classes were more like babysitting than Christian ministry. We often felt that while we told the kids the most extraordinary faith stories, we still were losing them. We were often frustrated: at one of our meetings I pitched the idea of teachers taking sabbaticals every year (with me being first in line since I'd been teaching the longest and had come up with the idea). We wanted the children to experience the direct love and acceptance of Jesus. More than anything, we prayed we would offer classes that the children really wanted to attend. And just when we got to the end of our rope, our minister found out about Mark Yaconelli.

There was an article in the paper about Mark's highly successful ministry with children and youth and his belief that children could be a part of—and, in fact, have—their own contemplative ministries. He was teaching teachers and kids how to develop skills to practice the presence of God. He taught teachers how to be with kids in ways that helped them believe that church was a safe place where they could feel fully alive, fully themselves, engaged, listened to, respected, and taught, even as they could impart to the teachers their own wisdom and perspective. He was teaching children and teenagers how to be *present* with each other, and with God, in ordinary times, in the midst of messes, and during big and small triumphs. He was making God real, vital, fun, true.

We arranged for him to sit in at our church school one day, and things have never quite been the same at Saint Andrew. He started working with children in our classes and in relaxed yet somehow intensive sessions with the teachers. We were invited to watch Mark work with teenagers, and I can honestly say that watching my son Sam get to know Mark has been an experience I cherish. Like every kid who has met him, Sam flipped for Mark. (In fact, one of their conversations is recounted on pages 205 and 206.)

Mark taught us how to listen. He taught us how to make classes something we all genuinely look forward to. He helped us become more confident as teachers and more understanding of the fact that the children and youth were teachers, too. He shared his deepest spiritual experiences with us, and received ours, with gentle respect. He taught us how to deepen—and help our children deepen—the direct, life-changing experience of the presence of God. There was, of course, always going to be some sense of us-against-them, but as Mark shared the great teachers and writings and voices of Christianity with us, and with the kids, he made the material feel fresh and new again for the teachers and utterly amazing for our students. Instead of us giving our positions on God and the Bible and spirituality, Mark showed us how to offer young people a chance for authentic spiritual understanding and growth, a chance for joy and safety.

I am so grateful to him—especially for helping my own son look forward to Sundays.

If you are a church school teacher—or a regular parent interested in teaching your own kids—you will find in these pages a wise and patient teacher with a reverence for God, a deep respect for kids, and a lovely sense of humor. You'll find wonderful, hands-on stories about Mark's work with young people, Christian Ed leaders, his father, and his own children. There are fantastic tried-and-true exercises for breaking the ice, focusing, and being playful as a group.

Through it all, you will find Mark Yaconelli—and if you are any-thing like me, you'll find direction and validation and a lot of truly great suggestions in his words.

Finally, I want to promise you that if we can do it at Saint Andrew, you can do it, too; and we are doing it now with a much happier sense of purpose, together, on Sunday mornings.

—*Anne Lamott*

# Acknowledgments

Since 1993 I have spent hundreds of hours in small circles of people praying, listening, and discerning God's presence within churches and youth ministry programs. This book is an attempt to put into words the experiences and wisdom I've gained from these little communities of faith.

My first thanks go to the youth who accompanied me as I sought to discover a new way of approaching youth and ministry. Many of these young people were my first teachers in discovering a new way of being with God and others. I'm especially grateful to the youth of St. Andrew's Presbyterian Church in Portland, Oregon; Novato Presbyterian Church in Novato, California; and Sleepy Hollow Presbyterian Church in San Anselmo, California, for their patience and friendship as I came to them again and again saying, "We're going to try a little experiment..."

I extend my heartfelt gratitude to the adults with whom I ministered in each of these congregations. Special thanks go to Hal Iverson, Terrie Carpenter, Nancy Wiens, Leona Davidson, and Jeff Fletcher from Sleepy Hollow who taught me a great deal about ministering as a spiritual community.

The Program in Christian Spirituality and the Diploma in the Art of Spiritual Direction at San Francisco Theological Seminary transformed the way in which I approach God, myself, and others. I'm especially grateful to Sister Elizabeth Liebert who continues to be a great mentor, teacher, and friend. Thanks also to the PCS community during my years at SFTS—particularly Sister Mary Rose Bumpus, Rebecca Langer, Ann Pope, and Joan Currey. Our weekly meetings of prayer, sharing, discernment, and planning were invaluable in modeling a new way of working within a religious institution.

This book and the years of research and experience that it rests upon would not have been possible without the foresight of Chris

Coble and the generous support of the Lilly Endowment. Chris saw the potential of contemplative youth ministry long before I did. The subsequent grants given for the creation and support of the Youth Ministry and Spirituality Project allowed these ideas to come to life within youth rooms, congregations, and youth ministry institutions across North America. This book is yet another fruit of that investment.

My soul's gratitude goes to the spiritual directors, scholars, interns, staff, and advisors who served within the Youth Ministry and Spirituality Project—especially Paul Bock, Nancy Wiens, Daniel Wolpert, Garry Schmidt, Teresa Blythe, Diana Cheifetz, Doreen Kostynuik, Chip Laird, Suzanne Buckley, Dina Gardner, Scott Hardin-Nieri, Carol Hovis, Marie Pappas, and Kay Collette, who were involved in several events and consultations. The wisdom and guidance these spiritual friends provided within the YMSP transformed me as well as the participants in the project. Special thanks go to the project "consigliore" Frank Rogers, whose friendship and guidance has gently tended the work of the Youth Ministry and Spirituality Project, this book, and my life.

I am forever indebted to the youth directors, pastors, churches, denominational leaders, and youth who participated in the Youth Ministry and Spirituality Project (1997-2004). The transformation we experienced together was a sign of the reign of God. Special thanks go to Tammy Clark and Jen Butler as well as the church leadership and youth ministry communities at Valparaiso First United Methodist Church in Valparaiso, Indiana, and Westminster Presbyterian Church in Eugene, Oregon, respectively, whose commitment to prayer and youth ministry served as a beacon within the project. (You can find interviews, testimonies, practices, and reports from the folks who participated in the project at *www.ymsp.org.*)

I extend thanks to Marge and Doug Frank and their colleagues at the Oregon Extension in Lincoln, Oregon, who granted my family and me a place of rest, retreat, and reflection where this book could come to life. Thanks also go to Kirk Wulf, Deborah Arca Mooney, Cory

Maclay, Jen Butler, Frank Rogers, and Jay Howver who read and "contemplatively" critiqued the first version of this manuscript.

I'm grateful to Kathy Helmers who was a great help in interpreting the publishing world and securing a safe port for this book. Thanks also go to Doug Davidson, whose clear, concise, and heartfelt editing made this work much stronger than I could've imagined on my own.

I'm indebted to Andy Dreitcer for his companionship in co-founding and co-directing the Youth Ministry and Spirituality Project (1997-2000). Andy's wisdom and mentorship were invaluable in the development of my own understanding of contemplative ministry. I carry deep gratitude for Michael Hryniuk, who served as Co-Director of YMSP from 2001-2004. Michael's friendship, prayer life, patience, and laughter are woven within my life and work.

Deborah Arca Mooney served as program manager for the YMSP and has been administrative assistant, spiritual director, youth leader, janitor, secretary, cheerleader, nurse-maid, travel agent, proofreader, counselor, concierge, van driver, ego masseuse, and mother superior not only to the participants of the project, but most especially to me. I cannot imagine engaging in this work over the past eight years without her care and friendship.

The love and acceptance of Morton Kelsey (1917-2001), my friend, teacher, and spiritual grandfather, continue to reveal to me the companionship of Jesus.

In 2003 I suffered the loss of my dad, Michael Yaconelli, who was a great playmate, soul-friend, and colleague. He has been the inspiration for much of my life and ministry and was a great supporter of my exploration of contemplation and ministry. This book is both a response to and a continuation of his life and work.

My heart's gratitude goes to my family—the little spiritual community that lives with me, eats with me, carries my burdens, celebrates my breakthroughs, offers me forgiveness, and enlarges my soul.

Noah, Joseph, and Grace, you are my greatest delight. Thank you for your patience while I typed on the computer.

Jill, my one true love, thank you for carefully reading and editing this book, as well as most everything I've written since I was 18 years old. I know it's possible to be lovingly and truthfully present to others because I continue to receive this from you. My heart is yours.

# introduction: practicing the presence of Jesus

The more we receive in silent prayer, the more we can give in our active life. We need silence to be able to touch souls. The essential thing is not what we say, but what God says to us and through us. All our words will be useless unless they come from within. Words which do not give the Light of Christ increase the darkness.

—MOTHER TERESA OF CALCUTTA

Young people just can't have somebody reciting lines or reading a book or teaching. You want someone who's learning, someone who's alive and growing with you. That's how you learn that you're on a spiritual journey with somebody. It doesn't work if that adult is at the end of the journey tugging on a rope trying to get you to come along. A young person needs to know you're right there with them. A young person needs to see that you're vulnerable—that you're struggling too. I have to say I haven't seen a single adult enter our youth ministry and leave the exact same way they entered. Everybody has changed…and that's just how it's got to be.

—NATHANIEL, AGE 15, ATLANTA, GEORGIA

Youth are not blank slates, and Christianity is not words. That may seem obvious until you seek to share the Christian faith with young people. Then you may notice your first impulses involve words. "What will I say? What books should I read? What answers will I give? What discussion should I evoke? What blanks within young people need filling?" In sharing the faith with youth, most of us think about the words and the empty spaces. If we go to seminary or step inside a Sunday morning worship service, we're immersed in words. A newcomer to these settings might easily assume Christianity is words. It's reading, memorizing, lecturing, preaching, and writing. It's books, newsletters, worship bulletins…Words, words, words.

But the central problem in sharing the Christian faith with young people doesn't concern words; it's deeper than that. The real crisis facing those of us who seek to share faith with youth is this:

We don't know how to be with our kids.

We don't know how to be with ourselves.

We don't know how to be with God.

*We don't know how to be with our kids.* We know how to entertain them, market to them, test them, and statistically measure them. But we've forgotten how to be with them. As a result today's youth have become more and more isolated, alienated, and left to fend for themselves within the molesting arms of the corporate media culture. This isn't just my opinion—it's the conclusion of every major study on adolescent development over the past 15 years.[1] Consider the words of Cara Miller of the Search Institute, possibly the largest researcher of adolescent development and behavior in North America:

> Study after study in the field of youth development
> makes it clear that the single most important
> thing that can make a positive difference in the

[1] Almost any study done in the past 20 years on adolescent health and religiosity makes this claim. See Hurt, Chap Clark, Baker Academic, 2004; or the recent work of the National Study of Youth and Religion, particularly *Soul Searching: The Religious and Spiritual Lives of American Teenagers*, Christian Smith with Melinda Lundquist Denton (Oxford University Press, 2005).

life of a young person is the presence of a caring adult. In spite of that, research shows that most young people don't have enough caring adults in their lives.[2]

Sadly, our absence from the lives of young people is connected to a deeper problem: *We don't know how to be with ourselves.* Most adults are busy. We have no down time. We move from activity to activity, with few real relationships and little introspection. We're "distracted from our distractions by our distractions," to paraphrase T.S. Eliot. The result is that we've become "dis-spirited." We live narrow lives. We tend to act as if we're nothing more than our roles and our jobs. We become what Thomas Merton calls "the false self." Anthropologist Angeles Arrien relates that in many indigenous cultures, a dis-spirited or dis-connected person is diagnosed by asking four questions:

Where in your life did you stop singing?

Where in your life did you stop dancing?

Where in your life did you stop telling stories?

Where in your life did you stop listening to silence?

When I look at the world around me, I see very little singing that isn't play-listed, very little dancing that isn't connected to soft-drinks, very little story-telling that isn't violent and disjointed, and a complete absence of silence. The sad truth, if we're willing to be honest, is that youth are being raised in a culture of people who no longer live from the center of their lives. The results are catastrophic for those of us who tend to the spiritual lives of teenagers. Anyone who befriends young people knows they're people of spirit—people drawn to song, dance, story, and silence. We cannot hope to touch the hearts of youth if we have lost our own spiritual rooting.

[2] This summary was in the 2004 spring newsletter of the Search Institute. For more information by the Search Institute see *www.search-institute.org.*

In the Christian community there is an even deeper block: *We no longer know how to be with God.* In the church we love to debate God, defend God, protect or promote God. We talk to God, praise God, and even serve God. The one thing for which we have little time or patience is actually spending time with God. If you're a pastor in a church, one sure way to get fired is to set aside 10 minutes of silence during a worship service for people to just "be" with God. Try this a few times and soon the church leadership will be inviting you to just "be" somewhere else.

Increasingly, it appears as if we in the church have forgotten how to be in relationships—which is tragic, since our primary calling as Christians is to be people of relationship. Jesus calls us to love God with all of our hearts, minds, strength, and spirit and to love others as we love ourselves (Mark 12:29-31). Most youth ministers are drawn to this work by a deep ache to live as spiritual people and to share the life of Jesus with teenagers. In order to be spiritual guides, we have to spend time in the Spirit. We have to slow down and live at "God's speed." We have to be patient. We have to give ourselves permission to pray, to listen to people, and to be humble and willing to wait on the Holy Spirit to lead the way. How can we share God if we're too busy to be with God? How can we love kids if we aren't present to them?

In contrast to our lives of spinning isolation is Jesus' life of relationship and presence. Jesus' presence, his capacity to love and be with people, is transformative. You can see it in the way he listens, shares food, spends time, weeps, walks, touches, responds, and cares for others. Jesus enjoys being with people. He enjoys being with God. His ministry, it seems, doesn't come from a pre-planned formula but instead arises in response to the real situations and relationships he encounters.

If we want our young people to live lives of faith, we need to live into the presence of Jesus. If the Christian faith is to offer any light, love, or truth to young people, we have to move beyond words. We have to share not only the teachings of Jesus but more importantly the presence of Jesus.

What does it mean to be present? It means being open and available to others with as much of ourselves as possible, as unguarded as possible. To be present is to be awake to the Mystery of God within each moment. It means relating to youth in the way Jesus related to people—with authenticity and transparency.

Jesus is generous, patient, kind, welcoming, courageous, truthful, and compassionate. Jesus is available to people. He is attentive to God and to others in the present moment. He receives people. He has patient eyes that see people in their beauty as well as their pain. Jesus trusts people. He trusts our capacities to bear love. He trusts us with the good news. He trusts us with life. He trusts that we know more of God than we realize. He says, "I no longer call you servants, I call you friends." He doesn't say, "Let me explain." He says, "Remember." He says, "those with hears to ear…" He says, "A sower went out to sow…" He says, "Listen."

The best way to know the presence of Jesus is to turn to him ourselves. Who would we become if we spent time in the presence of Jesus? How would we live if we spent long periods of time with someone who trusts us, enjoys us, listens to and cares for us? Who would our youth become if they were companioned by adults who embodied such love and attention?

Most of us can't answer these questions because we have rarely experienced such presence in our own lives. If we added up the amount of time spent in the presence of another person who truly listened and cared for us, it might equal less than 30 minutes. Yet Jesus demonstrates that this kind of patient presence is possible—and then goes on to tell us that we have the capacity to share this kind of

contemplative youth ministry

presence with others. He calls us to love one another—and for young people today (and all of us), love means being there.

Unfortunately, the last place many teenagers find people open and available is within churches. Instead of a listening ear, they find advice. Instead of a witness to their lives, they're offered programs and activities. Yet we know that the people who've had the greatest impact on our lives, the people who have changed and shaped us, are the people who were present to us—people who received us in the midst of our pain as well as our breakthroughs.

If we want our kids to grow into themselves, to be people who know how to offer God's love, life, and creativity to a brutal, hurting, and stunted world, then we need to share the presence of Jesus with them. We need to remember how to be in relationship with young people.

# A Contemplative Approach to Youth Ministry

In recent years there has been a rediscovery of the significance of presence within the Christian life. Locked away within ancient books, monastic communities, and the lives of individual praying Christians is a deep concern for presence—presence to God as well as presence to other people. This yearning to be fully awake and alive, the desire to be attentive to others, the longing to be receptive to God's call in every moment of our lives is the heart of the contemplative tradition.

Contemplation means "being" with God within the reality of the present moment. Contemplation is about presence. It's about attentiveness—opening our eyes to God, ourselves, and others. Contemplation is an attitude of the heart, an all-embracing hospitality to what is. Contemplation is a natural human disposition. It's the way in which we approached the world as children: vulnerable, open, and awake to the newness of the present moment.

We've all experienced being contemplatively present. Even as our adult minds become distracted and burdened with worry, we still receive times of contemplation, times of simple presence. These are unrehearsed moments when a deep sense of gratitude falls upon us and we find ourselves without need or want, satisfied and reverent at the Mystery of life. They are moments when we feel surprisingly alive to the people and situations before us. Like love, contemplative awareness is not something we achieve; rather it comes as a gift, simply to be received.

Ignatius of Loyola referred to contemplation as "seeing God in all things." Brother Lawrence called it "the pure loving gaze that finds God everywhere." Jean Pierre de Causade defined contemplation as "the sacrament of the present moment." Teresa of Avila referred to this experience as "Awareness absorbed and amazed."

My favorite description comes from Walter Burghardt, who said contemplation is "a long loving look at the real." In contemplative youth ministry we look, long and lovingly, at what is. Contemplative youth ministry is about courageously beholding the reality of our own lives, the reality (whether it be joy or suffering) of the young people we serve, and the reality of God's love beneath it all.

These definitions of contemplation, I believe, are descriptions of how Jesus was present to others. He engaged people with openness and honesty, unafraid to take "a long loving look at the real"—at the people and situations he encountered.

Contemplative youth ministry is an invitation to slow down and receive the young people in our lives. It's a reminder that what youth need most are people who know how to be present to God and present to others. What would it be like if our ministries were filled with adults who took a "long loving look at the real?" How would our youth respond if adult Christians engaged them with patience and transparency? What would it mean for our own lives if we could become people who sought to be present and receptive to what God brings us in life instead of hurriedly striving toward the next task or project?

To be attentive to youth and aware of God in the present moment is always a struggle. We live in a complex age that demands that we multi-task. We grow up trained to attend to many commitments at once. Our minds and imaginations often drift toward the future or dwell in the past. Yet is there any greater gift we experience in this life than that of another person's full attention? Is there anything more loving than to be fully seen and heard by another? Didn't most of us become Christians when we sensed that God was present to us?

Contemplative youth ministry isn't just another ministry model; it's an opening of the heart, an attentiveness to God, a receptivity to the Holy Spirit, a growing relationship with Jesus and his way of compassion. Contemplative youth ministry isn't about becoming mystics or turning kids into cloistered monks and nuns; it's about helping kids become alive in Christ. It isn't about candles and labyrinths; it's about youth and adults becoming present and available to God's love.

Contemplative youth ministry honors the desire to listen as well as teach in our interactions with kids. It grounds our ministries in prayer as well as evangelism—in silence as well as acts of justice. Contemplative youth ministry is about refusing to be so busy that you overlook God in your ministry. It's about remembering that Jesus goes before and beside us.

The contemplative tradition of the Christian faith comes to us as a precious gift in an age when no one has time to sit still. It comes as a medicine to a church culture obsessed with trends, efficiency, techniques, and bullet-point results. It comes to us just as Jesus approached his disciples in the midst of a busy ministry, asking them to "come away for awhile." Contemplative youth ministry is about trusting unashamedly that God desires our presence more than our activity. It involves recognizing that unless we find rest in God, we'll continue to live lives among youth that are harried, depleting, and in direct contrast with the life we seek to share.

The ideas and practices presented in this book do not come from detached study; they emanate from my relationships with young people, parents, youth ministers, and congregations across North America. For seven years I was given the resources from the Lilly Endowment and San Francisco Theological Seminary to create and co-direct the Youth Ministry and Spirituality Project (YMSP). The YMSP was formed in 1997 to participate in the renewal of youth ministry in the Christian church. Its mission is to foster Christian communities that are attentive to God's presence and discerning of the Spirit, so that these communities might better accompany young people in the way of Jesus.[3] From 1997 to 2000, we gathered a diverse group of churches from across the United States to see what would happen when contemplative prayer and presence was intentionally practiced within ministries with youth. These 16 churches and the people who represented them came from 10 denominations encompassing socioeconomic, ethnic, cultural, and geographic diversity. They also spanned diverse theological backgrounds—from conservative evangelicals to Roman Catholics to liberal Protestants.

Over the first three years of the project, we held four, one-week sessions in which we immersed pastors, youth pastors (both paid and volunteer), and at least one other adult from each sponsoring church in many of the principles and practices found in this book. We also held a one-week contemplative formation retreat involving youth from the participating churches.

[3] For more information, testimonies, and resources from the YMSP, see *www.ymsp.org*.

From 2000-2003, we trained a group of leaders from 13 exemplary churches as well as the national youth ministry officers from 10 denominations to become teachers of contemplative youth ministry. The churches and institutions were asked to integrate contemplative youth ministry into their ministries and organizational structures and to begin to share the insights of contemplative youth ministry within their respective communities. It has been an enormous privilege to work with so many diverse and gifted congregations. This book is an attempt to pass on some of the insights and transformation that flowed from our efforts to explore a different way of sharing Jesus' message of love with young people. At the beginning of each chapter and within the text I've presented just a small sampling of the stories, testimonies, and practices that grew out of the Youth Ministry and Spirituality Project. I urge you to read these quotes and stories as if you were listening to a dear friend. Pay attention to the words or images that stand out to you. See if you can sense the transformation that these parents, youth pastors, church members, and pastors have undergone as they've begun to listen more deeply to young people and to the presence of God in their midst. Similarly, I've included many of the exercises and contemplative processes tested within the project. I hope you'll take time to engage the exercises and practices as they are presented in this book—these experiences are critical to understanding the message of this book.

Although I've spent 16 years studying, teaching, and practicing youth ministry, I must confess that I was never involved in a youth ministry program when I was an adolescent. The church I attended as a young person was small and rural. It had neither a youth group nor Sunday school classes. What it did have, however, was a time during each worship service in which people were invited to stand and greet one another. This time of greeting was always (and still is) the longest period of the service, as people took the time to hug and converse with every other person in the room. Each Sunday, whether I was sulking in the back row, hiding in the kitchen, or immersed in my conversations with friends, people found me, asked how I was, listened to my words, and hugged me to their chests. I know I'm a Christian today because those people were present to me during my adolescence. They listened openly to my questions, received me, looked at me with wonder, and saw within me a unique revelation of the presence of God.

This book is born of my hope to provide every young person with a handful of adults who incarnate the love, compassion, and presence of Jesus in a similar way. I pray that our churches might be filled with adults willing to move beyond words and ministry programs—adults willing to take the time to seek out the young people in their communities, to sit with them, to listen to them. May every congregation be filled with adults who view the young people in their lives and communities with the eyes of Jesus, beholding in each and every one of them a unique revelation of the presence of God.

# teen angst and adult anxiety

# 1

In our age everything has to be a "problem." Ours is a time of anxiety because we have willed it to be so. Our anxiety is not imposed on us by force from outside. We impose it on our world and upon one another from within ourselves.

Sanctity in such an age means, no doubt, traveling from the area of anxiety to the area in which there is no anxiety or perhaps it may mean learning, from God, to be without anxiety in the midst of anxiety.

—THOMAS MERTON, *THOUGHTS IN SOLITUDE*

I've really begun to understand what deeply spiritual people teenagers are. (Silly to have forgotten, when I was one myself.) Even the scruffiest middle-schooler is on a seriously beautiful, completely unique journey, as we all are, and have been, even when we were little kids. Understanding that has perhaps been the best fruit that contemplative prayer has yielded in my relationship with young people.

—MELISSA RANGE, POET, YOUTH MINISTRY VOLUNTEER, OAKHURST BAPTIST CHURCH, DECATUR, GEORGIA

Teenagers make adults anxious. They just do. In fact, adult anxiety about teens may be the primary reason youth ministry exists.

Spot a cluster of unfamiliar young people laughing outside the church, and adults get suspicious. If these youth happen to paint their lips black or jump skateboards off the church steps, adults can get downright fearful. Adult anxiety toward teens is ancient, even biblical. In the only scene we're given from Jesus' adolescence, the young Messiah sneaks away from his family and hides out in Jerusalem. When his mother finally rushes into the temple and discovers her holy middle-schooler, she cries frantically, "Child, why have you treated us like this? Your father and I have been searching for you in great anxiety!" (Luke 2:48). It turns out that even the teenage Prince of Peace can make adults crazy with worry.

There are many reasons why adults feel anxious around teens. Young people are fidgety. They fiddle with things and won't stay still. They exaggerate and mirror adult postures that make us self-conscious and uncomfortable. They always seem to be looking for something—a friend, an adventure, a ride, food, acceptance, a glimpse of who they're becoming. Youth can voice their questions with such open-hearted honesty that we find ourselves blushing. Sometimes their neediness or suffering can be obvious in a way that leaves us feeling helpless or despondent.

Young people are green. They can make adults feel tired, musty, and unattractive. Emerging from childhood, teens move toward adulthood with fresh eyes and energy. They see white elephants. They ask the obvious and un-faced questions: "Why do we have to go to church when Jesus never did?" "How come you tell me not to drink alcohol when you have a beer every night?" "Why are these benches called pews?" Just the presence of young people within a community of adults exposes weaknesses, raises doubts, and challenges assumed values.

teen angst and adult anxiety

Young people can be disturbingly (or is it refreshingly?) unpredictable. One day they seem happy to conform to their parents' wishes and adult conventions; the next day it appears they're making it up as they go along, led zigzag by an internal drummer that even they don't seem to recognize. Young people can express a childlike dependency one moment, then get offended by the lack of independence they're granted the next. Youth are messy. Take this example:

Three years ago while traveling on a bus full of young people, I noticed I was seated near five or six teenage girls. At the time, my wife and I were expecting our first daughter, and I was eager to learn about the relationships between these teenage girls and their fathers. I asked the girls if they would be willing to tell me about their relationships with their fathers and to offer any advice they thought helpful. Although these young women were from all over North America and represented diverse ethnic and racial backgrounds, I was surprised at how all the girls in this particular group spoke in very similar, adoring tones about their dads. Then one 15-year-old said, "Of course, you have to be prepared for times when your daughter might say to you, 'I hate you, Daddy!' But usually by the next day you'll get a handmade card that says something like, 'You're the greatest dad in the world.'"

Bewildered, I looked at her and asked if any of them had enacted this kind of behavior with their own fathers. All but one nodded in agreement. I was incredulous. I asked what had prompted them to use such extreme language. One girl replied, "Well, it can be anything, really. Like, a couple of months ago I stopped talking to my dad after he wore black socks and sandals to pick me up from school. But other times I've said similar things for really no reason at all." When I asked them why, they just shrugged their shoulders. "It's just something we do," one of them offered. Youth make adults anxious.

One thing that becomes increasingly disturbing for many grown-ups is the sense that they have little control over young people. This scares adults. Adults want youth to conform to adult standards. They want kids to act responsibly. They want them to sit down and listen. They want them to hurry up and get their identities fixed and grounded. Adults want youth to have a roadmap for a secure and reasonable future, and they get rattled when they notice that most youth aren't carrying one.

Youth workers aren't immune from these anxieties. We worry about the young people in our care. We don't know what they look at on the Internet. We can't keep up with the electronic gadgets they play with. We've never heard of the bands or celebrities they talk about. We don't know what they do after school. We're unaware of the subject or codes in their e-mail conversations. Even the most hip youth ministers can sometimes feel like they really don't understand young people at all.

Perhaps one source of these adult anxieties is the growing separation between youth and adults. For the past 40 years, economic policies, changes in social norms, and a relentless marketing strategy to create and sell to a teenage market have combined to create what sociologist Christian Smith calls a "structural disconnect" between adults and youth.[4] This separation begins long before adolescence. Many youth spend most of their childhoods segregated in daycares and schools, afternoons and evenings in front of televisions and computers, weekends hanging out with friends. By early adolescence most young people are attuned to a different reality, a different world, than adults.

The less contact adults have with young people, the more mysterious they seem. Adults can fall into the traps of projection, speculation, worry, and fearful imaginings. Congregations and church leaders find themselves relying on the media to learn about kids. They absorb stories about teenage gangs and violence. They watch videos and movies that portray youth as hormone-driven, sex-crazed nymphs. They hear news stories and government reports that talk alarmingly about "at-risk" kids. All of this becomes a filter for how young people are

[4] *Soul Searching: The Religious and Spiritual Lives of American Teenagers* (Oxford University Press, 2005), 182.

perceived. Adults see teenagers in baggy jeans and oversized jackets and fear they're hiding drugs or weapons. They see a group of young women in short halter tops and lipstick and worry about their sexual activity.

Sadly, most adults are unable to see the truth—that drug use and sexual promiscuity among youth have continually decreased over the past 20 years. So much so that Bill Strauss, co-author with Neil Howe of *Millennials Rising: The Next Great Generation* claims, "Never before has there been a generation that is less violent, less vulgar, less sexually charged than the culture being offered them." We fail to recognize it's the adult culture that is far more "at-risk" than the youth culture. Strauss claims, "We need a youth committee on adult drug abuse, not the other way around." But many of us believe the story the media and culture tell us about youth. We don't take the time to get to know our youth as they really are. Instead we view them through the media lens. We see them not as our children, or even as people; we see them as a dangerous tribe, a marauding cluster of "at-risk" statistics evoking fear and apprehension.

Sometimes adult fears about youth arise from what we *do* know. Adults get scared when young people reflect behaviors and attitudes we recognize. Adolescent desires for pleasure, material goods, entertainment gadgets, constant activity, sex, and mood-altering substances all mirror the behavior of the adult culture—and it scares us. There is much we adults don't like about ourselves. There are mistakes parents have made and want their kids to avoid. We get frightened when youth begin to reflect the ambiguous values and conduct of the adult culture.

I remember the mother of a teenager in my church youth group who was terrified her daughter was going to start smoking. She brought her daughter to church hoping she would get involved with "good" kids and healthy activities. This mom questioned me obsessively after every retreat and camp event to see if her daughter had been smoking. The reason she was scared? She had started smoking in high school and even as an adult was unable to stop the habit. Often the things we adults fear most in our youth are the issues we haven't resolved in ourselves. Thomas Hines, author of *The Rise and Fall of the American Teenager*, writes that we fear youth because "we want them to grow into healthier, wealthier, and wiser versions of ourselves." When they don't appear to be on that path, adults get scared.

Maybe what's most unsettling about youth is the way in which they remind many of us of our own adolescent hearts. Young people can stir up forgotten dreams and evoke unmet longings within adults. They can unearth the contradictions between the hopeful vision of our younger selves and the mediocre and muddled reality of our adult lives. Whatever the particular cause, the truth is that when adults relate to teenagers out of anxiety we miss seeing them, we miss hearing them, and we lose our sense of compassion for them.

Anxiety is the inability to be present. It's a state of agitation in which we lose our larger capacity to empathize, to love, to respond to the needs of others. When we're anxious we become squirrel-like—nervous and wary, teeth chattering, eyes scanning for danger, muscles spring-loaded, waiting to scamper up the nearest tree at every sound. Anxiety comes from words that denote "to choke." When we're anxious we can't breathe. We feel life closing in, leaving fewer and fewer choices. We find ourselves unable to discern real fears from reactive worry. We lose patience, and we're unable to trust. We get suspicious, distancing ourselves from others, ourselves, and even God. We become lost in our heads, caught up in fearful thoughts and calculations. Our minds oscillate between the future and the past. We worry about what should have happened or fear what might take place. In anxiety we lose touch with what's driving us. Our actions become self-protective, reactive, and compulsive.

It would be an overstatement to say that anxiety is the only adult response to young people. There are many instances when a young person's presence can be an unexpected grace that lifts a grown-up's spirit like a sudden gift of flowers. Youth can be unabashedly friendly and welcoming in a way that wipes away the clouds of mistrust or dourness many adults live behind. Youth are often playful, drawing energy and new life to the surface of adult lives and communities. Young people can be passionate about God and ultimate meaning in a way that elevates or even carries the faith of those around them. They can embody a heartfelt compassion for suffering and marginalized people that is revelatory to adults. They can ask the hard questions that help adult communities see hidden problems or possibilities.

There are many more positive ways, not to mention ordinary ways, in which adults respond and relate to young people. Yet the primary reaction to teens within Christian communities and the culture at large seems to be anxiety.

As a result most youth ministries in North America are ministries of anxiety. In fact, most Christian communities don't even consider the spiritual needs of young people until there's a critical mass of anxious adults. Look behind most youth ministry programs and you'll find pastors and church boards nervous about declining memberships, parents afraid their kids lack morals, congregations worried the Christian faith has become irrelevant to younger generations, and the persistent frustration among adults that something ("anything!") needs to be done with "those kids!"

## Teen Angst

Of course, adults aren't the only ones with anxieties. Perhaps the second most common reason youth ministries exist is that teenagers have their own anxieties about adults. Adults make teenagers anxious. They just do.

I once asked a group of graduating high school students to give me their impressions of adulthood. For the next hour kids shared their observations and experiences with parents, teachers, and various adults in the community. As the discussion began to wind down, I handed out paper and pencils and asked the kids to craft a one-sentence definition of adulthood based on our discussion. The room was silent for a minute or two, as the youth wrote and reflected on what they had heard. I then asked the young people to share what they had written. The first young man to respond said, "Well, as I heard our conversation and thought about my own experiences with adults, I wrote this definition: 'Adults have no friends, adults have no passions, and adults are stressed out.'"

Adults have no friends, adults have no passions, and adults are stressed out. In a single sentence, this young person was able to articulate the fear I have felt among most young people during my 15 years of youth ministry. More and more it appears to me that this definition represents the nightmare of adulthood most young people are trying to escape. Is it any wonder there are 30-year-olds still living in their parents' house, still trying to make it in a rock band? Maybe they're trying to hang on to their friends. Maybe they're trying to keep their passions alive. Maybe they see the grey-suited adults working in cubicles, burdened with responsibility, and they get frightened.

Young people are about energy. They have bodies that want to move, they have emotions they want to express, and they have developing relationships that are incredibly interesting and important to them. Adults—especially in a faith community—are about status quo. They want young people to listen, to behave, to be still, to stop talking, to soothe adult fears, to fulfill mission statements, and to support programs. This makes young people wary and anxious.

I once interviewed for a youth ministry position at a church in which part of the interview was done by a group of young people. When I asked what kind of youth ministry they envisioned, they said things like, "Something that's not boring." "Lots of trips and retreats." "We want to be able to hang out with friends." "Lessons about real stuff we care about—not just what adults care about."

As they continued to talk, I sensed that their comments were rooted in their fears about the church.

- Fear that the church wants youth to be passive.
- Fear that youth programs will be about meeting the needs of the adults.
- Fear that the real purpose of youth ministry is to make youth "nice."
- Fear that the youth ministry will be a form of babysitting.
- Fear that there will be only talking and no action.
- Fear that the ministry will be another activity in which youth have no voice.
- Fear that the ministry will have nothing to do with real life.
- Fear that they will have to hide their real thoughts, fears, desires, and experiences.
- Fear that youth will become as muted, controlled, and stressed as the adults in the congregation.
- Fear that there is something in Christianity that really matters, yet it will remain hidden.

The anxieties and fears young people hold regarding adults and churches are real. Yet ministries that respond only to teenage anxiety will mimic the media's frenetic activity that seeks only to keep the attention of young people, without any concern for the growing hunger of the adolescent soul.

# God Makes Us Anxious

For many adults, there's an even deeper anxiety than the ones I've mentioned—and it has a profound effect on our ministries with youth. It's the very real fear that the Christian faith is really about risk, about breaking free, about becoming vulnerable to the suffering in the world, about living as an open-hearted person.

A few years ago I was invited to a session meeting for a local Presbyterian church to talk about youth ministry. Instead of my normal presentation, I asked the adults to tell me why they started coming to church. Surprisingly, I found that almost all of them began attending church after they had children. They began attending church because they thought it would be good for their kids. They wanted the church to help their kids learn the values and morals of the Christian faith. As we talked further, we realized all of them were repeating the practices of their own parents. All of the session members were raised in families that began attending church when the children were young and then left the church once the children reached late adolescence. I asked how this had affected them. There was silence. Then one adult said, "Well, it didn't have much of an effect…except once I became parent, I thought I should probably start taking my kids to church."

I suggested that simply taking their kids to church or youth group would probably garner the same results. I explained that the purpose of youth ministry isn't just to help young people learn morality, as important as that is; it's to help them enter into the alternative way of life that Jesus offers. It's to help young people unmask the principalities and powers that seek to bind us—to help them live in freedom. It's to help youth learn the practices, understandings, and disposition that will keep them close to the Source of life revealed in Jesus Christ.

"Well, that's all well and good," offered one parent, "but I think that's more than we're after." Heads nodded around the room. "I think we just want our kids to, you know, learn the Ten Commandments and be kind to others—the kind of values Jesus was promoting."

"Yes," chimed another session member, "We don't need our kids to be Jesus, we just want them to participate in the church."

I paused and then told them that if they wanted their kids to learn morals, they probably could just take them to a scouting program. I asked if there was a deeper desire within their decision to bring their kids to church. I tried to explain that the purpose of the church was to help people live the Christian faith and that the Christian faith wasn't focused on morality. I tried to explain that the Christian faith is about following Jesus; it's about falling in love with God. It's about seeking to become so transparent to the Spirit of God that you are no longer sure which actions are your own and which ones are God's. I tried to explain that youth ministry isn't really about church memberships— it's about helping kids live in the freedom and compassion of Jesus. I tried to explain that morality was simply a by-product of loving God and bringing that love out into the world!

I sensed the adults were curious, but didn't know how to respond. People looked down in embarrassment. I became embarrassed. The pastor cleared his throat and in a voice that hinted "Okay, we've had enough out of you!" he said, "Yes, terrific! Thanks so much for your words of encouragement. I think we're done here and need to move on to the next item on the agenda." He then stood and escorted me to the door.

Sometimes it's difficult for us to admit that Jesus came to offer us another way of life—one that involves more than being a good citizen, obeying the law, recycling your garbage, and attending church on Sunday. Although many adults try to ignore Jesus' life of passionate freedom and relationship, youth are drawn to it.

Years ago as I tucked my sons, Noah (age four) and Joseph (age two), into bed, I was singing them a song I had learned as a boy that contained the word *Christian*. Noah asked, "Dad, what's a 'Christian'?" A sudden panic came over me. This was an important opportunity to share my faith! I needed to proceed carefully. I reviewed all the strategies in which I'd been trained. Testimony? No, too long. I'd risk putting him to sleep. Exegesis on Philippians 2? Might be too heady. Plus, I'd

*[handwritten margin note:] The purpose of the Christian life...*

contemplative youth ministry

40

have to go into a historical-critical description of Pauline theology, not to mention the concepts of kenosis and atonement. Maybe a brief historical sketch of the council of Nicea, culminating with a pictographic version of the Nicene Creed? Could be complicated.

My son interrupted, "Well, Dad, what does it mean?"

Before I could gather my thoughts, I found myself blurting, "Well, Noah, it means 'little Christ.' People who are trying to live like Jesus call themselves Christians."

Noah paused, pondered this definition, and then said, "Are you a Christian?"

"Yes I am," I replied.

Noah stood still, thought for a moment, and then said, "How do you become a Christian?" I explained that you simply say to God with all your heart, "I want to join Jesus in loving you and loving others," and then you try to live your life like Jesus. Noah thought this over and then said, "Okay. Let's do it." We sat together on his bed and prayed a simple prayer while two-year-old Joseph jumped and tumbled behind us.

The boys brushed their teeth, listened to a bedtime story, and climbed into bed. Soon they began to drift into slumber. As I got up to leave, Noah said to me, "Dad, I don't think I want to be a Christian." I paused, surprised he was still awake.

"Why is that, Noah?" I whispered.

"Well, Jesus gets killed by the soldiers doesn't he?"

"Yes...he does," I said hesitantly. Then with calm assurance I offered, "But God raises him and his Spirit is still with us today."

"I know that Dad...but I don't want to get killed."

Silence. "Don't worry," I said, rubbing his back, "you're not going to get killed. That happened a long time ago."

He yawned and with his eyes closed said, "Yes, but if Jesus is still with us today, it can happen again." Pause. Yawn. "I don't think I want to be a Christian, Dad."

"Okay, Noah," I said, brushing his hair. "Okay."

Noah realized that being a Christian has consequences. That living a life of love often results in suffering. That being like Jesus doesn't mean simply being nice and having good morals—it often means facing the pain and evil in the world. And I realized that night why many people resist the real purpose of youth ministries. That night I wasn't sure if I wanted my kids to be Christians—to "pick up their cross and follow Jesus."

I understood that night why many adults and youth simply want youth ministries that provide morals and safe social activities, without all the weird stuff about growing in the image of Christ. It's difficult for parents to trust their children to God. Look what happened to Jesus! Look what happened to the disciples! Look what happened to his friends, those we point to as saints! Parents, church members, and youth might want Christian values and assurances, but we don't want the life of Jesus.

Jesus makes us uncomfortable, causes us to question our daily practices. Jesus' life reminds us of the realities of suffering, hostility, hatred, and resistance that often accompany any attempts at living in truth and love. When kids learn to live in the Spirit of Jesus, they may no longer fit in. They may become outcasts. They may develop a costly compassion for others. They may become more vulnerable to the pain and loneliness of the world. They may be drawn to live life on the margins.

Being a Christian isn't safe. You can lose your life. You can lose your reputation. You can lose your relationship with a loved one.

Yet as I reflected on my interaction with Noah, I realized there is a worse fate than facing the suffering and violence of this world. More than I want to keep Noah safe from harm, I want Noah and all of my children to live. I want them to become fully alive. I want them to know Jesus so they will know how to keep their hearts soft. I want them to know God so they'll be intimately connected to the Source of life. I want them to be Christians so they'll know how to give and receive love—so they'll avoid the burned-out life of materialism that deadens spirits and kills creativity. But I have to admit, all of this scares me at some level.

A friend of mine who is a youth minister and a committed Christian called me one evening after receiving a phone call from her college-age son. She sounded distressed as she told me her son had decided to leave his studies to join a group of Americans going to Iraq to be with Iraqi civilians during the U.S. bombing and occupation. The group hoped that by being a visible presence as American citizens they might be able to protect the lives of civilians, as well as increase awareness about the suffering of Iraqis back in the States. My friend was upset and told her son he had made a commitment to college and this was no time to engage in radical politics. I asked how her son responded. She sighed, and there was quiet over the phone line for a moment. Then she answered with a sob in her voice. "He said, 'But Mom, this isn't politics. This is about following Jesus. We're going as a Christian group. Didn't you and the church teach me that Jesus was always befriending people who were weak and suffering?'" I waited in silence. I could hear her crying. Then finally she said, "He's right, you know, Mark. I know he's right. But if I knew he was going to do something like this, I would've taken him out of the church and raised him to be a Chippendale dancer."

# Rooted and Grounded in Anxiety

In response to the anxiety of adults (they're the ones with the power, after all!), most congregations create youth ministries that are about control and conformity. When we're anxious, we want control, we want answers, we want concrete and measurable results. We want our ducks in a row. In youth ministry this means most adults want programs and professionals. Church leaders want experts and predictable systems that will remove the doubt and ambiguity surrounding most interaction with young people. Congregations want discipleship formulas that will guarantee their kids will become moral and faith-filled believers.

When youth ministry responds to the anxiety of adults, it becomes restrictive and deadening. God's freeing presence and the at-risk life of Jesus are downplayed. Kids are taught to conform to the tradition, practices, and doctrines of the congregation. Soon the youth ministry loses its ability to discover something new, to question and embrace the pain and suffering of life. The ministry becomes safe, revolving around answers and false assurances. The youth are quarantined. They're placed at the margins—incubated in basements or gathered at off hours when the congregation won't be disturbed. The ministry becomes more and more unreal, causing those young people who won't conform to become disruptive or swallow their real questions and struggles.

Other youth ministries are created in response to adolescent anxieties. Noticing young people's discomfort with adult forms of faith and desperately seeking to keep youth engaged, some churches develop ministries of distraction. Inspired by parachurch youth ministries from the 1950s, like Youth for Christ and Young Life (whose founder, Jim Rayburn, once wrote a book entitled *It's a Sin to Bore a Kid*), ministries of distraction keep youth moving from one activity to the next: rafting trips, pizza parties, game nights, ski retreats, beach fests, music festivals, amusement parks, taco-feeds, scavenger-hunts,

contemplative youth ministry

crowd-breakers, raves, skits, and whatever other activities attract kids. It's a Nickelodeon approach to youth ministry that seeks to appeal to kids' propensity for fun and recreation. This is how churches respond to youth who cry "Church is boring!" It's the ministry of excitement; discipleship through fun, culture-friendly, "Christian-lite" events. Like parents who pop in a video to entertain the kids when relatives arrive, the idea is to keep the young people from running out, to keep them in the general vicinity of the church, to keep them happy until they're mature enough to join the congregation.

While such ministries may keep youth entertained, they often keep youth distracted from the deeper rhythms and practices of the Christian faith. Programs and activities are chosen based on the level of excitement that's generated. No one wants to act like an adult for fear of scaring the kids. Leaders become hesitant to engage youth in any activity that is in contrast to the consumer culture. Prayer, spiritual exercises, theological conversation, and spiritual disciplines that challenge the status quo are dumped out of fear that youth may cry "This is like school!" or "You're just like our parents!" or (worst of all) "This is boring." So the ministry never addresses the deeper needs of youth, never challenges them to explore the alternative way of Jesus. Like children's television programming that seeks to keep kids attentive so they'll watch the commercials, our ministries of diversion respond to young people's most carnal appetites so we can slip in a five-minute Bible study or parade them through the church building.

Ministry programs that respond to the anxieties of adults or youth are incapable of awakening kids to the freedom of God. Rather than trusting the presence of God, these reactive ministries put their faith in attendance, conversions, and confirmation class sizes. To get the necessary results and to assuage fears, they become more and more about control and manipulation. Kids know, even when they can't articulate it, when a ministry is concerned with control and manipulation. They know when the purpose of the ministry is to alleviate fear. They know when ministries are simply about protecting young people from the realities of life.

Once young people recognize that youth ministry is really about quelling anxiety one of two things can happen. If the ministry is uninteresting or provides few social opportunities, the young people will eventually leave. If the ministry provides youth with fun outings, entertainment, and occasions to socialize, kids are happy to play along and ease the fears of the congregation. They assent to being paraded in front of congregations ("Don't worry, the church isn't dying!"), doted on by congregational leaders ("No fear! Your financial allocations are producing results!"), and photographed for the church newsletter ("Have no doubts, Christianity is alive and well!"). As long as there are trips to Disneyland, church dances, and the annual summer Jamaican mission trip, they're happy to pretend. Just don't expect them to be around once they leave high school—or when the program budget dries up. That's when they'll have to get on with the real stuff of life.

# life without expectations

# 2

Religion is not **our** concern; it is God's concern. The sooner we stop thinking we are the energetic operators of religion and discover that God is at work...so much the sooner do we discover that our task is to call people **to be still and know**, listen, hearken in quiet invitation to the subtle promptings of the Divine. Our task is to encourage others first to let go, to cease striving, to give over this fevered effort of the self-sufficient religionist trying to please an external deity. I am persuaded that religious people do not with sufficient seriousness count on God as an active factor in the affairs of the world. "Behold, I stand at the door and knock," but too many well-intentioned people are so preoccupied with the clatter of effort to do something for God that they don't hear Him asking that He might do something **through** them.

—THOMAS KELLY, *A TESTAMENT OF DEVOTION*

You don't have to fix things. God is already there. You just have to be open to God's love and transparent to what God is doing.

—ALEXX CAMPBELL, AGE 18, SAN ANSELMO, CALIFORNIA

The anxieties present in youth ministry are not an abstraction to me.

I was 25 years old, newly married, and in my first full-time job as a youth pastor at a mid-sized Presbyterian church in Portland, Oregon. The congregation had just completed a 12 year campaign to build a new youth facility with a large multi-purpose room and two youth classrooms.

Although this was my first paid job in youth ministry, I felt experienced and well trained. My father, Mike Yaconelli, was considered one of the founders of youth ministry in North America and owned Youth Specialties, a company that produced workshops, conventions, and publications to train youth ministers. I had attended these events since I was a toddler, and had spent countless hours among teens and highly capable youth ministers. I had a library filled with the latest curricula, exercises, and models for sharing the Christian faith with young people.

So it was a surprise when, after two and a half years in the ministry, I realized I was a failure. The signs were obvious. When I was hired, there were approximately 10 teenagers involved in worship and Sunday school. At that time the church leadership gave me a list of almost 50 teens from church families who were uninvolved in church activities. In my first few months at the church, many of these families had me over for dinner or met me after worship and introduced me to their children. The expectation was clear: I was to find a way to get these kids involved in the church and form them in the Christian faith. Yet despite doubling the number of youth events, increasing the youth budget, and working 70 hours a week, the youth program appeared stagnant under my leadership. It seemed the only kids interested in church or the Christian faith were the 10 who were already involved when I arrived—and sometimes even they didn't show up.

Parents and other church members began to express frustration that I wasn't attracting more youth to the church. Most of the young people in the congregation seemed to be avoiding me. I was called in to talk to the personnel committee who asked for a better description of how I spent my time. Other youth directors in the area expressed surprise when I showed up to regional gatherings with only two or three kids. "Aren't you Mike Yaconelli's son?" they would ask. "Where's the rest of your youth group?"

Each week there was a public ritual that highlighted my failure as a youth pastor. In order to encourage more youth to attend Sunday morning services, the Christian education committee had created a "youth pew" where young people were invited to sit together during worship. Of course, the youth pew was in the very front row, visible to the entire congregation. Each week I was expected to sit with the youth as the designated host and chaperone. I began to dread Sunday mornings. I would wait until the last possible moment and then, while the congregation was standing and singing, I would slink up the side aisle and take my assigned seat. I often sat nervously perspiring, waiting to see if some teenager would join me. In reality, I wasn't sure what to hope for. To be alone in the youth pew was a public sign that kids didn't want to hang out with me. On the other hand, to sit helpless while two or three disinterested kids slept, punched holes in the church bulletin, or removed the stick pins from the designated visitor ribbons and pierced their palms like Cheyenne warriors was a painful sign of my ineffectiveness.

I began to suffer more and more anxiety. I felt like a fool, embarrassed to admit the job was too much for me. I wanted desperately for the kids to like me. I wanted to meet the expectations of the church leadership. I wanted to create a bold group of teenage Jesus-lovers. I wanted to quell the frustration of tithing parents. I wanted to live up to my dad's reputation. I wanted to fulfill my own images of success.

Instead, I suffered insomnia. I couldn't sleep more than a few hours a night. My wife hardly saw me. I tried to burn my anxiety by putting in more hours. I would leave home at seven in the morning to drive the school bus routes, offering kids rides; then I'd spend evenings attending high school sporting events or phoning various teens to try to coax them to attend Sunday school. I spent weekends helping out at other Christian youth programs—hoping their kids might come over to our church. I volunteered in schools across town and spent afternoons handing out hot chocolate at bus stops. But nothing seemed to work.

I even tried to bribe kids. I provided donuts and caffe lattes at morning Sunday school, and cookies and soda at each youth meeting. I picked kids up during the school lunch break and took them out to their favorite fast-food hang-outs. The youth seemed wary and unrespon- sive. They liked the treats but expressed no interest in the Christian life or the church. No matter how many young people I contacted during the week, the same 10 kids showed up for every Sunday school class or youth event. I finally fell into a depression when it occurred to me that the kids who were participating didn't care about the time and effort I was putting into the program. They just liked being together—and planned to show up whether I was there or not.

When my wife expressed concern about my long work hours and nights away from home, I responded with irritation. Didn't she realize I was doing God's work? Wasn't it clear I was seeking to save the souls of the youth in the community? Couldn't she see I was failing? Didn't she realize I was going to have to work harder to share the good news? Didn't she remember that Jesus was killed doing the very same thing? Wasn't it obvious I was going to have to suffer trials and tribulations in order to get these overscheduled, middle-class teenagers to see the significance of the Christian life?

Of course, underneath my anger and frustration was a sickening suspicion that my ministry to teenagers was stagnant because my faith was weak. I committed myself to becoming a more effective Christian.

I bought a devotional book and spent an additional hour each morning in prayer and Bible study. I prayed for each kid in the church by name, pleading with God to increase the number of youth in the program—or at least motivate some kids to become followers of Jesus. Surely these acts of devotion would convince God to bring me success!

Instead, the numbers dropped. Soon I had only a handful of kids attending Sunday school and youth group programs. I began to suffer dizzy spells. The low point arrived when only one kid signed up for our annual summer camp—a camp I'd spent hundreds of hours planning and organizing with four other churches. I began to feel there was nothing I could do to please God, the youth, or the church. I became resentful. I began to tell myself that the Christian life was too heavy and burdensome and that I was not cut out to do ministry. I became withdrawn from my wife and friends.

Looking back, it's easy to see that this whirlwind of effort wasn't really about the Christian life. Although I believed I was trying to help young people discover Jesus' way of love, in reality I was more worried about meeting expectations. My driving concern was to please kids, please parents, please the church, and please God. I desperately wanted to meet those exterior expectations so I would know I was worth something—so I could mitigate my inner fears that I was a failure as a disciple and a human being. The ministry was just a means of seeking tangible proof that I was loved by God—or at least by young people. Thus, the focus of my ministry wasn't God's love, but rather, my own anxieties and expectations, and those of all the other adults in the church. And the kids could smell it.

Sadly, this kind of anxiety is a common motivator within North American Christianity, often masking itself as spiritual passion. I recognize this same anxiety to succeed among many pastors, parents, and Christian outreach programs directed at youth. It's a drivenness to perform, an obsession with results, a concentration on goals and outcomes that discounts the ordinary graces and small cries for mercy inhabiting our daily lives. Deeper than that, such driven ministries point to a God who appears as a distant ideal or a set of principles, a stern moralizer full of demands and expectations. Our anxiety-filled ministries expose an unspoken belief that God is utterly untrustworthy, that God's impotence has forced us to take responsibility for the souls of young people ourselves.

Of course, this is in complete contrast to the patient trust and downward mobility of Jesus. Unlike the efficiency experts populating North American Christianity, Jesus wasn't focused on abstract goals and principles. Jesus seemed to be a person deeply concerned with the small picture. He seemed content to receive the people and situations directly in front of him. He seemed satisfied that trusting God and others in the present moment was enough to communicate the reality of God's life. Jesus' ministry lacks anxiety—despite the fears of the disciples, the incredible needs of people, and the vindictive anger of those in power.

Fortunately for me, there was an associate pastor at the church who was seeking to carry the same trust Jesus embodied. Through regular meetings and conversation, we developed a friendship, and I learned to trust his insight. One day he invited me to attend a retreat led by an Episcopal priest and author, Morton Kelsey. I was reluctant to attend; it seemed an inefficient use of my time when I had hundreds of youth to save. I bowed out, blaming the high retreat fee and my lack of transportation. But my friend knew I needed some time away and, without my knowledge, applied for a scholarship on my behalf. One week later he informed me that my fee had been paid, and he would drive me to the convent each day so I could attend the sessions. I was out of excuses and reluctantly agreed to go along.

The conference was held at the Franciscan Renewal Center, a former convent that the few remaining sisters had refurbished and were operating as a retreat center. The first session was on a Monday night. As soon as we entered the room, I wished I hadn't come. It was a small, pastel-tiled gymnasium. The walls were partially covered with pock-marked, sound-proofing tile, much of which was dissolving into tired brown cardboard. On one side of the room were 40 or 50 metal chairs set out on various colored carpet pieces. Grey partitions were placed along the back row to create a make-shift enclosure. After appraising the setting, I scanned the participants. It was my most feared combo: white-haired ladies and overly friendly pastor types peppered with wall-flowers, loners, and introverts scribbling in bloated notebooks. Except for one woman in her late 20s, I was the youngest person there by 25 years.

We took our seats, and one of the sisters came forward to lead us in a song. It was immediately awkward. Without instruments to guide us, the melody was elusive. Half the group remained silent while the other half overcompensated with voices that could exorcise the Christian faith from Mother Teresa. I stood and quietly mouthed along while the aging sister sang. For the rest of the week, she began each session in the same way. I still remember the words:

> Open my eyes, Lord.
>
> Help me to see your face.
>
> Open my eyes, Lord.
>
> Help me to see.
>
>
> Open my ears, Lord.
>
> Help me to hear your voice.
>
> Open my ears, Lord.
>
> Help me to hear.

Open my heart, Lord

Help me to love like you.

Open my heart, Lord.

Help me to love.


I live within you.

Deep in your heart, O Love.

I live within you.

Rest now in me.[5]

After we sat down our host offered some staff introductions, explained the schedule, and introduced the retreat speaker. Seventy-year-old Morton Kelsey reminded me at first of the scarecrow in *The Wizard of Oz*. He was tall, gangly, and presented a long narrow face grooved with smile lines. He wore a plaid western shirt with a bolo tie and wobbled when he walked, like a man stepping off a freighter after a season at sea. Thick black-rimmed glasses held his eyes, and bulging flesh-colored hearing aids hung on each ear. Morton took his time making his way to the front, steadied himself, then panned the room with such a broad goofy grin that I was certain he'd wandered away from a nearby nursing home.

When Morton spoke, his voice was gentle, slow, and sing-songy. Words were rounded like the speech of the partially deaf. His manner was comforting and wholly unintimidating. At times he would

life without expectations

say something that struck him funny, causing a great gasping sort of laugh that set us all off-guard. Other times he spoke of his encounters with suffering with such stillness that you could feel the emptiness within him. I remember listening to him speak that first night as if the world were enchanted and infused with the possibility and presence of God.

That night and each subsequent morning Morton gave a meditation on a parable. Most of them were from Luke 15 (the lost coin, the lost sheep, the prodigal son). He spoke of the spiritual reality these parables revealed—a reality of love and mercy that he claimed was more real than the limited win-lose world of consumption most of us inhabited. Although his ideas were illuminating, it was the place from which his words arose that I found most striking. Morton seemed to speak from the inside. There was a knowing, an experience of God, that carried his words to the door of the heart. Although he was highly educated, when he spoke of God's love, it wasn't out of study or prescribed doctrine. He seemed to speak from something he'd seen with his own eyes, heard with his own (broken) ears, touched with his own hands, and felt with his own heart. I began to sense that for Morton, God was not a moral principle or a heroic ideal, but rather a very ordinary and living presence—a presence that, through the life of Jesus, seemed to offer a boundless, shameless kind of love each and every moment.

After each talk Morton invited us to engage in some sort of spiritual exercise. Throughout my upbringing as a Christian, I had engaged in numerous "faith-building" exercises. Most were educational drills that relied on study and discussion to help assimilate spiritual or religious information. Yet the exercises Morton prescribed were different, for they were primarily invitations to *encounter* God. They relied not on words, study, and reason, but on silence, prayer, and imagination. I later discovered that many of those exercises are part of the ancient and forgotten contemplative prayer tradition within the Christian church. Rather than treat God as a means to an end, these disciplines and exercises invited one to "be" with God, to move inside and seek the presence of God without expectation. This was new to me, and in direct contrast to a Christian upbringing that, until then, was focused on words, moral principles, and good works. It had never occurred to me to actually seek to be with God, to open myself to God without an end in mind.

On the third day of the retreat, we were asked to imagine ourselves in the story of the prodigal son—allowing ourselves to see, hear, and feel the events of the story as if we were present. The group dispersed and each person was instructed to find a quiet, solitary place to pray. Immediately I went to my friend and asked if we could leave early. He was a little surprised, and then told me he had committed to helping the staff that day and couldn't take me home. He asked if I was going to do the prayer exercise. I replied that I understood the basic meaning of the exercise and didn't feel the need to waste time doing it. He shrugged his shoulders, mumbled, "Well, I think I'll give it a try," and walked off.

Feeling a little admonished, I resigned myself to enter the prayer. I walked down to the basement of the building and found a small prayer chapel. I set out my Bible, read the parable, and then closed my eyes and waited, allowing the story to take place within me from beginning to end. At one point in the silence, I felt a tangible and disarming sense of welcome. An overwhelming reality of love and acceptance poured into each of my senses, leaving me shaking with tears and filled with a deep sense of rest.

When I got control of myself, I exited the room, certain I was experiencing some sort of psychological breakdown. The experience had been so ultra-real that I suspected the months of anxiety about my ministry and faith had finally split me open. I knew Morton was trained in psychotherapy, so I approached him quietly at the end of our next gathering and asked if I could speak with him alone. That night after dinner we skipped evening vespers and found a small classroom away from the group. I told him about my experience in prayer—the sense of love and acceptance, the outpouring of tears, and the deep sense of relief. I also told him of my months of anxiety and asked him if I was having a nervous breakdown. Gently, he asked questions about my family life, my work situation, and my upbringing. With each story I shared, he would respond by telling pieces of his own life history—often sharing experiences similar to my own. I soon noticed how calm I felt as we discovered similarities in our relationships with our fathers and our work within the church.

After a couple of hours, we were winding down. Morton rose and put on his jacket. I panicked for a moment, realizing my question hadn't been answered. I blurted out, "So am I having a breakdown or not?"

Morton paused, smiled at me, and then said, "Well, what do you think? You seem calm, comfortable, and open. Do those seem like the signs of someone having a breakdown?" I had to admit I was feeling a sense of rest and relief that was new and attractive. He said, "Mark, my guess is you had some encounter with God's love, and maybe now you can believe God has no expectations of you."

I tried to let this sink in. We walked to the door and Morton gave me his phone number and address. He told me he'd be available any time I wanted to talk, day or night. "But," he said, "only call if you want to." I nodded my head. He looked at me again and said, "It's up to you. If you wish to talk more, I would be delighted to carry on our conversation. But if I don't hear from you, I will be glad we had this time and won't be upset or worried in any way." I nodded a second time and started to thank him for the time. He gently grabbed my arm to stop me and said a third time, "You understand that if you contact me, I will be happy to talk. But I will be equally satisfied if you never contact me again."

Finally, it struck me what he was trying to communicate. My throat tightened. He then said, "You see, I'm trying to tell you I have no expectations of you. Just as God has no expectations of you. God offers love to you, just as you are. I have enjoyed our conversation and I am open to whatever happens after this. It's up to you." I looked down and nodded, my eyes heavy with tears.

Three days later I entered the junior high youth room at my Presbyterian church filled with a new source of energy. I had come in contact with the reality of God's presence in the world—and it had changed everything. It was as if the scales had dropped from my eyes. Suddenly I was filled with questions: If God is alive and present, then how is God moving within the ministry? If God is so available, then how is God present to each of these kids?

Almost overnight, the ministry no longer seemed to rely on my skills. It no longer seemed to be about my anxious attempts to attract kids or conjure up God. Instead, I realized my role was secondary. I realized God is the deep reality of life, not just a hope or ideal. God is alive and actively inviting each young person into a relationship of love. I realized my role was to get out of the center, to let God do the ministering, and to help youth notice and name God's presence in their daily lives.

It occurred to me then that the failure or success of the ministry had never been in my hands. Suddenly I felt I could relax. I could release my tight hold on the outcomes of the ministry and instead seek simply to be faithful, open, and present to God and the young people.

That's similar to the way Jesus shared his faith. Jesus was open and available...present and trusting...patient and waiting...confident he didn't need to control or manipulate anyone. Jesus trusted that his presence—his prayers, words, silences, and acts of love—would be enough.

staying alive

3

The adults who make Christianity come alive are the adults who take an interest in me—the adults who show an interest in my life as well as a passion and interest in their own lives. Not only do they say, "Hey, how are things going with you?" They're also willing to sit down and say, "Let me tell you what's going on with me." Those are the people I really enjoy. Those are the people who have kept me in church.

—NATHANIEL, AGE 19, EUGENE, OREGON

The glory of God is manifest in the person fully alive.

—IRANAEUS OF LYON

contemplative youth ministry

In a recent survey, parents were asked to share their most important goal in raising children. The most common response was "to raise a moral person." In order to attain this goal, many parents take their children to church.

Adults don't want kids to get into trouble. Parents want their children to be safe from bad kids and bad deeds. Church members want youth who are courteous and respectful. Adults want kids to do as they say and not cause problems. Parents want their kids to make them proud and avoid embarrassing misbehavior. If I were to put into words the most immediate, surface question many parents have when they bring their kids to church, it would be this: "Can you help me keep my child safe and good?" *wow,*

I was invited to a meeting at a local church to talk about youth ministry. Parents and other church members were distressed that young people had stopped attending, despite the church's investment of time and money into an activity-packed youth program called "Youth Power!" Instead of discussing the specifics of the youth program, I asked people to tell me why they wanted kids in church. People were startled at first and looked at me as if the answer were obvious. Then they began to respond. One man called out, "Church is good for kids."

"Can you be more specific?" I asked.

"Church is where kids learn values and morals," he responded.

Then a mother spoke up, "I want my kids involved in the church so they can get involved in something positive. I don't want them getting into trouble or hanging out with bad kids."

Most of the remaining comments echoed those sentiments. I stopped the discussion and said, "I have a recommendation. If your primary reason for wanting young people in church is to keep them moral and protected, then you should be upfront and tell them.

staying alive

I suggest you change the name of the youth group from 'Youth Power!' to 'Nice and Safe!'" The parents laughed, knowing none of their kids would be interested in a program that sounded so bland and protective.

After a pause, one father spoke up. "You know, I bet the reason our kids don't like coming to church is because they know it's all about us," he said. "They know that despite all the outings and activities the program is really about our desire to teach them to stay out of trouble." As this insight began to fill the room, many of the adults felt embarrassed at the exposure of their real intentions.

I reminded the group that it's good to want our kids to be protected and moral. I asked them, however, to take a moment to notice if there were any deeper desires they harbored for their children and the other youth of the church. I gave the parents a period of silence, urging them to simply rest for a while and then turn a simple awareness toward the depths of their hearts. I then asked them to see if they noticed words that helped express their deepest hope for young people.

The silence was rich and full. Some people's eyes welled up with tears. After a few minutes, I asked people to share what they'd noticed. Here are some of the responses I collected:

- My hope is that my daughter will know how much she's loved.
- I hope our youth can have a sense of God's joy and peace even in hard times.
- I want our youth to know they have a community of faith that will carry them.
- My hope is that our young people will live lives of love.
- I hope my children will know God is as close as their heartbeat, offering strength and comfort when they need it.

- I hope our kids will see Jesus as a friend, and realize they're not alone.
- My hope is that our youth will know they are not just consumers, or statistics, or employees—that they have gifts and abilities God has given to them. I want them to know they're uniquely made by God.
- I want our kids to know they belong to a long history of people who have followed Jesus in standing up to injustice and bringing light into the world.
- My hope is that our youth will have a faith that will help them know when the culture is trying to use or exploit them.

Take a moment to set down this book and prayerfully reflect on your own hope for young people. Gently and silently become aware of God's presence, and then simply ask, "What is my deepest hope for the youth I know?" Then wait. Don't force anything. Just see what words and images arise.

The Bible says people brought their kids to Jesus "to have him touch them" (Mark 10:13; Luke 18:15). I believe this same desire exists in the hearts of parents and congregations today. We want our kids to be touched. We want them to be blessed. We want them to make contact with the Source of life. We want them to know the freedom of Jesus. We want them to be alive as spiritual beings, despite the consequences and dangers in our materialistic culture.

As I consider my hope for my children and the youth I minister with, I am overwhelmed by a sense of gratitude. It's as if this hope is not mine, but rather something that has been given to me. The anxiety around my kids and ministry diminishes, and I am left with a paradoxical sense of deep yearning and deep satisfaction. I often ask workshop participants, once they've identified their primary hope for young people, to spend time in silent prayer asking God to make them aware of God's hope for young people. When I ask for responses, people generally notice that God's hope for their children is the same as or similar to their own. They realize their hope for young people is not something they created or made up; rather, it is God's hope. It is a gift, given to them to carry, to follow, to live by faith. "We hope for what we do not see," Paul says to the Romans (8:25).

Most of us have no clear plan for how to actuate this hope. We simply hope for things that seem unattainable—things we know not how to provide. Yet all the anxieties and fears around our young people seem to dissipate in the face of our unquenchable hope.

What is our hope for young people? We want them to live. We want them to be alive. We want them to be free. We want them to experience Jesus because we know, somewhere deep within us, that only God can keep them alive. We know it's possible to grow old without having lived. We know you can become so busy accumulating stuff, so distracted by the marketplace, so comfortable and insulated by technologies that you can miss your life.

*Beneath adult anxiety about young people is a real and persistent hope that youth will become fully alive and open to love.* Parents want their kids to live, to thrive, to experience joy, to create lives rich in relationship and possibility. It turns out that this same hope undergirds teenage anxiety about adults. Beneath adolescent anxieties about adults are more profound longings to experience lives that are passionate, meaningful, and full of deep connection to others. In fact, if I had to sum up the primary question youth seem to be asking in every interaction with adults, it would be this: "Do you know how to stay alive?"

Do you know how to stay alive? Beneath the anxiety, youth want to know how to live fully in this world. They are asking us: Do you

contemplative youth ministry

know how to become yourself despite the constant messages telling you that you're lacking? Do you know how to keep from becoming overwhelmed by the pain and suffering in the world? Do you know how to find a home, a place of welcome and relationship? Can you tell me how to stay hopeful and creative in a world obsessed with violence, death, and conformity? Do you know where I can offer my gifts meaningfully in a world that feels consumed with trivia? How do I stay alive? How do I remain open to God and others when so many people seem closed, distant, and angry?

Rarely do youth ask these questions so blatantly. More often they come embedded in questions concerning career choices. It's what they're listening for when they ask about our decision processes and learn how we made the transition to adulthood. Youth want to know why we believe in God. They want to know about our marriages or romantic lives. They want to meet our friends and find out what we do when we're not in church. They want to know what makes us angry and whether we agree or disagree with their parents. Behind these questions is a hunger to know how to live well, how to avoid the despair and sullenness that seems to possess many adults.

I believe our attempts to share the Christian life with youth must continually be measured according to how we respond to this question of becoming fully alive. The truth is that most of us who seek to share Jesus' life with young people are not great program administrators, entertainers, psychotherapists, or family counselors. We're not particularly skilled at designing exciting, educational curricula. No, the real gift we have to offer young people is this: We yearn to become fully alive. We long to live lives of deep connection. We struggle to resist our own damning, self-protective habits. We seek to live honest and authentic lives in a world fixated on pretending. We stretch toward God, the source of love, in the midst of the cynicism, materialism, and despair. We remember that Jesus said that our God is "not the God of the dead but of the living" (Matthew 22:32). As lovers of God, we want to be animated by that same life.

If we take the yearnings of young people seriously, then we can admit to ourselves that youth aren't interested in our answers (often given in response to questions they're not asking). They're not looking for safe activities. What they're seeking is the companionship of adults who embody a different way of being. They're looking for living adults who have room inside of them. Room for creativity and compassion. Room to hold the suffering and ambiguities of life. Room to listen and reflect on hard questions. Room to see the larger wholeness that exists beneath our fragmented societies. Youth are looking for adults who can guide them toward a different way of *being*, of living in the world. They are looking for adults who know how to live lives of love.

Ultimately as Christians, we trust that Jesus really is about becoming fully alive. We believe Jesus when he says, "I came that you may have life, and have it abundantly" (John 10:10). This is what Christians offer young people. Becoming alive is the Way of Jesus. This is the heart of our desire to share the Christian life with youth. This is the deeper purpose beneath our attempts to teach and model a moral life. This is why we want youth in worship. This is why we want to expose them to a Christian community. This is what motivates our youth programs and Sunday school classes.

Can we trust that our longing to become fully alive is a powerful gift to young people? Can we take heart that our desire for God will be enough?

# becoming a good receiver

# 4

You will discover that the more love you can take in and hold on to, the less fearful you will become. You will speak more simply, more directly, and more freely about what is important to you, without fear of other people's reactions. You will also use fewer words, trusting that you communicate your true self even when you do not speak much. The more you come to know yourself—spirit, mind, and body—as truly loved, the freer you will be to proclaim the good news. That is the freedom of the children of God.

—HENRI NOUWEN, *THE INNER VOICE OF LOVE*

Contemplative prayer has tamed my ministry of busyness. It has helped me recognize that even more than God needs me, God longs for me. With this new discovery, each encounter with young people is no longer an item checked off of the to-do list. I'm no longer seeking to earn more kudos from God (or better, my church!) The sense of Sabbath and the centering of the spirit that occurs in contemplative prayer reminds me that ministry is not a task that I do to or for others, but a gift I share in community with others.

—BRENT PARKER, SEMINARY STUDENT, YOUTH PASTOR, DISCIPLES OF CHRIST, FORT WORTH, TEXAS

For Jesus, becoming alive means becoming open and available to God's love. Jesus invites us to trust that underneath our anxious striving, beneath our worry and life-management strategies, there is the reality of God's love. I use the word *reality* because the church often thinks of "God's love" as referring to some future ideal, ecclesial principle, or sentimental hope. But this is a misunderstanding of Jesus' life. Jesus lives as if there is a boundless, shameless love present and available within every moment. His life is rooted in an unseen world more spacious and forgiving than the harried world most of us inhabit. Jesus lives a life that is grounded in love. Within the reality of God's love, people and situations appear different to Jesus. His eyes and ears notice things others seem unable to perceive. Through the presence of God's love, Jesus is able to feel and respond to the inner truth of each situation.

For Jesus, God's love and presence is tangible, intimate, and knowable. He knows that God's love is the source of our being and the endpoint of our deepest yearnings. Through his words and actions, Jesus communicates that this Presence of love can be trusted. Jesus seems to gently nudge us over and over to see, hear, and touch this love for ourselves. He wants us to open our eyes and see that God isn't an abstract belief; God is a present reality—available and trustworthy, offering us rest and inspiration. Jesus tells us the key to becoming fully free and alive is to participate in God's love: Love God with all your heart, mind, soul, and body; and love your neighbor as you love yourself.

For most of us this is not a new idea. We know we yearn for God's love. We know youth seek to receive and share God's love. Yet we're not very good at loving. Most of us have had poor models of love. So the question remains: How do we open ourselves to a life of love in the midst of an overlybusy, overstimulated, callous, and preoccupied society? How do we participate authentically in God's love in the midst of buzzing and blooming teenagers? Further, how do we help young people become aware of this love in their own lives?

One thing is clear: We can't create love. We can't conjure up God's love by offering kids sugary smiles and inspirational posters. Even if we seek to serve kids—help them with homework, drive them to and from school—our good acts can seem heavy and oppressive if they don't come from a spirit of love. We can't create more love for ourselves or for our kids; because the truth is, love can't be made, it can only be received. Love is a gift God offers to us, a gift that asks only that we let down our resistances and yield.

# Surrender

If love is a gift, then the first step in living into that love is to surrender. We need to stop trying to make kids love God (or make God love our kids). To carry the good news is to trust that God's love is present and available to our young people—even when our youth programs and ministries are neurotic, self-absorbed disasters. To share the Christian life with young people means to let God be God, and trust that our desire to share our faith will be enough. To surrender means to recognize that we don't control how God lives and moves. We don't control our churches. And we certainly don't control the spiritual lives of our young people. If Paul is to be believed, then we can assert that we don't even control ourselves: "I do not understand my own actions. For I do not do what I want, but I do the very thing I hate" (Romans 7:15).

Once we admit that we are powerless to turn kids into Christians, we can recognize that ministry is a series of small acts of trust. It's more about yielding to what is already present and available than it is about creating or building. If we can see we're not in control, maybe we can hear the truth that Mother Teresa once articulated—that in ministry we're "not seeking to be successful but merely faithful." The results of our labors are in God's hands. We can trust that our young people belong to God—that God has been seeking to love them since before they were born and will continue to love them long after they leave the influence of our ministries.

I have observed too many churches and youth ministries whose methods expose a consistent distrust of God. These ministries embody a sense of urgency that communicates a God who is either a relentless taskmaster or completely incompetent. This is the "functional atheism" of which Parker Palmer writes.[6] In youth ministry it appears as an endless parade of duded-up Christian rock stars, hyperactive activities, word-heavy programs, and teen devotionals covered in exclamation marks!!!!! There is a tangible sense that God must be dressed up or hidden behind high-energy music and charismatic speakers. Our churches and ministries seem deathly afraid of any kind of downtime. All silence and stillness is eradicated for fear that youth might find God disappointing, boring, or absent. It's as if our church and ministry leaders suspect God has left the building, and so they stall with jabbering words and meaningless activities in hopes the crowd won't become restless.

In contrast, Jesus isn't afraid of reality. He isn't afraid of doubts, or downtime, or disappointment, or boredom—in fact, I might even claim that he finds boredom, disappointment, and doubt critical to spiritual growth! He's not embarrassed or ashamed of God's presence—even when God appears ineffective in the face of great evil and suffering. Jesus loves the true, living, mysterious reality of God more than our names and images of God. He trusts that if we seek the truth of our existence, we'll discover the reality of God's abundant love. So Jesus urges us to stop. He invites us to come away to quiet and deserted places. He asks us to *be still and know.* He calls us to take a moment to do nothing. He urges us to turn our attention away from our anxiety and busyness and to simply to notice the work God is already doing.

becoming a good receiver

---

[6] *Let Your Life Speak: Listening for the Voice of Vocation,* (Jossey-Bass, 2000), 88.

When my wife was pregnant with our first child, she noticed she rarely felt the baby move when she was actively running errands and doing chores around the house. Only when she stopped, sat still, or lay down could she feel the baby's activity. Sometimes at night, I would have my own private moments with our unborn child. I would wait until Jill fell asleep, then I would reach over and place my hand on her stomach. I would lie there feeling the baby shifting and moving. I would sit in wonder at this growing person, stirring inside. Noticing God requires the same attentiveness. Unless we regularly stop our activity and sit still for a moment, we often miss making contact with the life waiting to be born. We miss God's Spirit moving within and around us.

When we stop all of our activity, we discover what is really driving our lives. To stop and surrender is to repent—to turn away from our preoccupations and remember the One who has gone before us. When we stay still, we become aware of the source of our activity—that which propels our ministries and relationships with young people. We can awaken to the real source of our faith, whether it is our own anxious fear or our hunger for God's love. We become available to receive the gift of love God has been waiting to give us.

## Receive

In order to live into God's love and create ministries that offer young people Jesus' way of life, we not only have to surrender, but we also have to be willing to receive. The Christian life begins by receiving. We don't know much about receiving in North America. For most of us, life is what you make of it. "What do you do?"—or for youth, "What are you going to do?"—is often the first question we ask when we meet someone. For too many of us, our response to this question becomes the basis of our identity. To live, in North America, is to do. The imagined purpose of life, both inside and outside the Christian church, is to become efficient and productive. Life is measured by the success of our individual efforts and ingenuity.

In contrast, a life of love is open-ended. Love isn't in a hurry to get somewhere; it doesn't live for the end result. Love takes pleasure in the here and now. Love seeks relationships. Love is not a means to an end. Love is its own reward. Paul writes that love is patient and kind; it bears all things, hopes all things, endures all things (1 Corinthians 13:4-7). If God is love (1 John 4:7-8), then these characteristics are not only descriptions of love, but also descriptions of the God who is alive and working within every moment.

Jesus is the best teacher of how to live a life of love. One of the most significant differences between Jesus and other people is that Jesus is a good receiver. He receives food from a cheating tax collector. He allows a prostitute to pour expensive oil on his feet. He lets children embrace him and people shout his praises. Most importantly, Jesus is willing to receive from God. When Jesus comes to the Jordan River to be baptized, the Scriptures tell us he heard a voice from God that said, "You are my son, the Beloved, with you I am well pleased" (Mark 1:11).

Most of us have heard many times that God loves and cherishes us. Yet how many of us really believe that? How many of us take the time to allow God's love to penetrate the depths of our being? How many of us believe that God only loves our good deeds, our self-sacrifices, our moments of prayer or devotion? How many of us are convinced God's love reaches us only when we say the right words and walk within the right lines? How many of us are driven by an unsettling anxiety that the Christian life is something one earns or achieves? Perhaps the essential difference between Jesus and others is that when he hears God call him "Beloved," he doesn't question it. He simply believes it. He receives God's name of love before he does any great works—before healing people, before speaking insights, before undergoing any sacrifices.

Jesus fully accepts that he is the beloved of God before he begins his public ministry. And this makes all the difference. Having received this love from God, Jesus is able to tolerate the doubts, false accusations, curses, and even hatred poured out at him—because deep within his heart, he knows and trusts the love God offers him. He knows within the marrow of his bones that he is beloved by God and that this is the deeper truth of his identity. Who would *we* be if we lived with that same knowledge? How would we interact with young people if we claimed our belovedness in God?

When we allow ourselves to be open and receptive to God's love and presence, we begin to notice that God is alive and available. We begin to perceive that the Holy Spirit is present and working beneath the worry and activity of our ministries. It may even occur to us that God has been present to our young people long before they met us—before they were even born. When we stop to receive God's life and love, we begin to understand that the Holy Spirit has been seeking our young people with greater passion and desire than we could ever work up. That's when it becomes clear that our ministry is really not about us. We notice a sense of relief that we're not the center of the ministry. We discover newfound energy as it dawns on us that our role in youth ministry is not to "make something happen!" Our task is to simply rest in wonder at what God is doing, and then to lend a hand as we're needed.

# allowing God to love us

# 5

My quiet time is the only place where I can just sigh and let my shoulders drop. I've come to a point in my prayer life that I no longer need to say anything to God or to perform a certain prayer. I can just sit there and know my intention to be in prayer is enough.

When I first started hanging out with youth, I felt I had to ask them a lot of questions, make jokes, and make them feel good. Now I plop down next to them and sigh and ask, "How are you?" Whether their response is a word or a five-minute monologue, I can sit with them knowing that my attention to them for that five seconds or five minutes is enough.

When I look back on my prayer life with God, I can't remember what we've said to each other.

When I recall the adults in my life who have shown me love, I don't remember anything they've ever said to me. I just remember that when we were together, one way or another they paid attention to me. Those memories of God and adults sustain me even to this day.

—ADAM YODER, YOUTH PASTOR, SEATTLE MENNONITE CHURCH, SEATTLE, WASHINGTON

Perfect love casts out all fear.

—1 JOHN 4:18

Changing the way we relate to young people isn't just a matter of developing new techniques or broadening our theology. It's about a different attitude of the heart. It's about being present to young people with a loving transparency. We're seeking to see teens with the eyes of Jesus, hear teens with the ears of Jesus, and perceive teens with the heart of Jesus.

The following list offers a very simple description of the different ways in which we go about ministry when we're rooted in anxiety rather than love. Notice the qualitative difference between a life and ministry based on patience and love, as opposed to one fueled by fear and anxiety. Although our ministries and actions are never this clearly defined, the following descriptions of these two dispositions point toward the kind of transformation we seek to undergo as ministers.

Anxiety seeks **control**.
(How do I make kids into Christians?)

Love seeks **contemplation**.
(How can I be present to kids and to God?)

Anxiety seeks **professionals**.
(Who is the expert that can solve the youth problem?)

Love seeks **processes**. *practices*?
(What can we do together to uncover Jesus' way of life?)

Anxiety wants **products**.
(What book, video, or curriculum will teach kids about faith?)

Love desires **presence**.
(Who will bear the life of God among teenagers?)

Anxiety lifts up **gurus**.
(Who has the charisma to draw kids?)

Love relies on **guides**.
(Who has the gifts for living alongside kids?)

Anxiety rests in **results**.
(How many kids have committed to the faith?)

Love rests in **relationships**.
(Who are the kids we've befriended?)

Anxiety seeks **conformity**.
(Are the youth meeting our expectations?)

Love brings out **creativity**.
(In what fresh way is God challenging us through our kids?)

allowing God to love us

| | |
|---|---|
| Anxiety wants **activity**. (What will keep the kids busy?) | Love brings **awareness**. (What are the real needs of the youth?) |
| Anxiety seeks **answers**. (Here's what we think. Here's who God is.) | Love seeks **questions**. (What do you think? Or as Jesus said, "Who do you say that I am?") |

We cannot undergo this transformation by the sheer strength of our will or intellect. Only by yielding can we even begin to embody the freedom of God. We have to let go and allow God to transform our anxiety into love. We have to allow God to show us a new way of being in the world, a new way of engaging in relationships with young people. We have to allow the Holy Spirit to teach us how to live from the heart instead of the head. We have to allow God to "de-program" us from habitually relating to kids as projects that need managing, rather than persons who need God's love and trust.

If we are to awaken young people to the reality of God's love, we need moments of open, receptive prayer. When we slow down and feel the life of Jesus in Scripture, we can't help but respond with wonder at his persistent vulnerability toward those he encounters, even in the midst of increasing rejection and impending violence. How does Jesus keep from reacting out of fear and stress?

In North American churches, we often overlook the way Jesus punctuates times of teaching, traveling, and healing, with "Sabbath" times of rest and prayer. It isn't some spiritual *machismo* or "other-worldly" martyr complex that permits him to embrace the suffering and hostility of humanity. It's his intimacy with God, his love-life of prayer, that sustains and grounds him. As ministers to youth, we too need time for communion with God. Our kids need us to sit silently within the wide field of God's love in which we "live and move and have our being" (Acts 17:28). They need us to spend quiet moments receiving God's Spirit so that, like Jesus, we might be infused with hope, compassion, and truthfulness.

Take a moment to set down this book and simply become aware of your surroundings. Allow your eyes to receive the light, colors, and shapes around you without seeking to "do" anything with what you see. Then gently close your eyes and turn your awareness to your ears. Allow yourself to receive the sounds and noises around you without judgment. Then take a moment to become aware of your body. Beginning with the top of your head, allow a gentle attention to move down your body to the soles of your feet. Allow yourself to notice places of tension or pain without passing judgment. Can you compassionately receive your physical self? Spend a few moments allowing your body, just as it is, to breathe and rest in the presence of God.

When you're ready, take a moment to direct your attention toward God. Quietly turn your awareness to the presence of God within all that you see, all that you hear, and all that you feel. Don't force anything. Just for a few minutes, allow yourself to open up to the presence of Divine Love within the reality of this moment—the way you might turn to receive the gaze of someone dear to you in the midst of a crowded room.

*meditation activity*

What was that experience like? Was it difficult to remain in silence? Did your mind become full of criticisms? ("I'm not doing this right!" "Nothing is happening!" "I hate these kinds of exercises.") Did you notice lots of commentary, day-dreaming, and analysis? Was the time restful or did it make you feel agitated? It's difficult to stop our activity and simply be present to God. The activity of our lives and the constant chatter of our minds make it challenging to simply sit in the present moment. This is true for everyone, even people who've spent most of their adult lives in silent prayer. Yet do you notice that this time of seeking to be present to God is also, in some inexplicable way, nurturing?

Prayer that invites us to dwell in the presence of God is called *contemplative prayer*. Some people call it "the prayer of the heart." It's prayer in which we allow ourselves to become open and undefended before God, to dwell within God's Spirit without expectation. It's Mary sitting at Jesus' feet, attentive and listening. It's Jesus resting in the boat during the storm. It's the psalmist who has learned to "Be still and know that I am God" (Psalm 46:10).

Although "contemplative prayer" sounds like a lofty spiritual exercise reserved for saints, in reality it relies on a simple attitude of the heart that all of us have experienced. The word *contemplative* means to "be in the temple." It means to rest in the temple or presence of God. When we seek to engage in contemplative prayer, all we're doing is seeking to rest attentively within the presence of God. Cistercian Abbot and author Thomas Keating writes:

> We may think of prayer as thoughts or feelings expressed in words. But this is only one expression. Contemplative prayer is the opening of mind and heart—our whole being—to God, the Ultimate Mystery, beyond thoughts, words, and emotions. We open our awareness to God whom we know by faith is within us, closer than breathing, closer than thinking, closer than choosing—closer than consciousness itself.[7]

Our human relationships involve times of talking, listening, and working together, but any long-term relationship also involves moments of simply resting in the presence of one another. This is the same disposition we seek to incorporate in our relationship with God.

---

[7] Cited in *Centering Prayer in Daily Life and Ministry*, Gustave Reininger, ed. (Continuum International Publishing Group, 1998) 130.

With three young and energetic kids, most of my time at home is spent helping with schoolwork, organizing schedules, playing games, preparing food, cleaning, and doing the errands and odd jobs that keep a household running. My wife's time at home involves even more of the same. Both of us seek to incarnate a sense of gratitude and love as we go about the mundane tasks of domestic living, but as any parent knows, domestic life can quickly make anyone fatigued and cranky. Over the years a pattern has developed where after the kids are asleep, Jill and I sit in the kitchen and spend an hour or two reflecting on the gifts and struggles of the day, just enjoying the pleasure of each other's company. These moments with my wife expand my life. They're moments when I can let go of constricting stress and allow my perspective to enlarge beyond my own frustrations and concerns. Many evenings after pouring out the events of the day or after sharing a particular experience of joy, frustration, or deep pain, my wife and I will simply fall silent. The silence may last a minute, or it may last a half hour. But in that silence, we dwell in the intimate presence of each other and the mystery of our lives—neither of us feeling the need to speak or act. I've noticed, over the years, that these moments of silence are often the most intimate and healing moments of our marriage. They're moments when we rest in the reality of our relationship (be it painful or peaceful), the relationship that is being woven together beneath our words and actions.

Contemplative prayer is an invitation to enter into a deep relationship with God. It's an invitation to set aside our agendas and spiritual striving and simply sit silently, vulnerable to God's presence within and around us. For the first 16 centuries of the Christian tradition, contemplative prayer referred to "resting in God."[8] We who seek to share the faith of Jesus amidst the energy of young people need this kind of spiritual rest.

Just like Jesus, our souls are drawn at times to deserted woodlands, quiet lakesides, and cloistered spaces where we can open our

[8] The term "resting in God" comes from sixth century mystical theologian, Gregory the Great.

allowing God to love us

hearts to God. Deep within us is a desire to share the life of Jesus—not just the words of Jesus. We seek time with the One Jesus trusted—the One who seeks to comfort our spirits, topple our barriers, arouse our generosity, and remind us of our larger capacity to love. We are made to commune with God, to breathe and live God. Our hearts, bodies, and souls yearn for space and time to sink into God's love where we might discover an underground reservoir of mercy. Those of us who seek to share the way of Jesus with young people need time to sit unguarded before the Spirit of God.

Over the centuries Christians have found many different ways to spend time dwelling in the presence of God. Some methods are unique to individuals; others have been practiced by groups and communities for centuries. For the past 12 years I've practiced and taught two basic, traditional forms of contemplative prayer to parents and people who minister with young people: *lectio divina* and centering prayer. After reading the descriptions of these prayer methods, take 10 minutes to engage in one of them before you continue reading. Give yourself permission to spend 10 minutes allowing God to minister to your spirit.

## *Lectio Divina*

*Lectio divina* is Latin for "holy reading" and comes out of the Benedictine monastic tradition. This prayer can be described as experiencing God through Scripture. It's a classical form of prayer designed to draw a person gently into the depths of her heart in order to meet God. For centuries lectio divina has introduced Christians to the practice of contemplation.

*Lectio divina* invites us into contemplative prayer by way of meditating on a particular biblical text. Before entering into the prayer, it's helpful to recognize that there are many ways in which we "read." We scan the newspaper for information. We study a book to increase our knowledge or hone our critical faculties. We become absorbed in a good novel. When we engage in *lectio divina*, we are not seeking to read the Bible for knowledge or instruction (although both of those may come), nor are we seeking the escape of a good story. Instead we come to the words of the Bible seeking to be with God. We come to Scripture as if it were a meeting place, a secret rendezvous where we hope to spend some time with the One who loves us.

My wife and I dated in college before the days of e-mail. During the summers, when we were apart, we would write letters to each other. I still remember the excitement of running to the mailbox after each workday, hoping to see a letter with my name written in Jill's handwriting. Each time I received a letter from my beloved, I would run down to my room, close the door, and then slowly pore over her words. When I read a letter from Jill, it was very different from other forms of reading. I wasn't seeking to catch up on the news as much as I was seeking to experience Jill. I was seeking to meet her in her letters, to receive her love, to feel her presence and be with her in some way.

When we engage in *lectio divina*, we come to the words of the Bible as if they are words from a lover. We come to the text seeking to encounter God, seeking to make contact with God's love and presence. We come to Scripture trusting God's nearness and God's desire to heal and transform us. We expect God to meet us just on the other side of Scripture.

The steps of this prayer might seem arbitrary and complicated at first. But as you engage in the prayer, you'll find the process is quite natural. (You may even notice you've practiced a similar form of prayer or Bible reading on your own.) The steps are as follows:

- **Preparation.** Begin by finding a passage of Scripture to pray with. You can choose a passage based on a lectionary, a daily devotional, or by simply selecting a passage on your

allowing God to love us

own. Make sure the Scripture is not too long. Next find a quiet place to pray where you won't be distracted or interrupted—a place where you feel safe and comfortable opening up to God. Often it's helpful to light a candle or set out a sacred object, something beautiful that quiets your spirit and reminds you of God's nearness.

- **Silence.** Once you've found a place to pray, take a moment merely to rest, relaxing into God's presence. With each breath become aware of God's love for you. Say a simple prayer offering yourself to God and welcoming whatever the Holy Spirit has for you.

- **Reading.** Read the passage once to get oriented to the text. Then read it slowly a second time, and a third, listening for a word or phrase that seems to shimmer or stand out in bold—a word that seems to address you. It may be a word that draws your attention through either attraction or repulsion.

- **Meditation.** Once a word or phrase has been given, repeat it to yourself, allowing the rest of the text to fall away. As you prayerfully repeat it, different thoughts, feelings, and images may arise. Allow this word to touch all that arises—thoughts, hopes, memories, images, and feelings. What do you notice? What is being offered?

- **Oration.** Let yourself express prayers of petition or gratitude as they arise. Your meditation on the word may uncover a place of pain or regret. Pray about it to God. You may notice a person or situation that needs prayer. Pray that to God, too. Honestly express your deepest thoughts, feelings, and desires in dialogue with God. Pray yourself empty.

- **Contemplation.** Finally, allow yourself to simply rest in God, like a child resting in her mother's lap. Lay down all of the insights, words, and images you've encountered and simply dwell in the presence of God. Sink into God beneath all your thoughts and feelings.

As you engage in *lectio*, you may find you prefer a different progression than the steps of prayer I've just laid out. For example, you may find yourself praying out all kinds of concerns at the beginning of the prayer. Or you may find yourself in a place of rest and trust after reading Scripture and then only find a word addressed to you from the text as you end the prayer. There's nothing wrong with that. "Pray as you can, not as you can't," Dom Chaplain once said. You're merely seeking to come to the Scripture with an open heart, seeking to be with God. You read the words of Scripture. You rest for a period of time. You leave with a word addressed to you. The prayer is that simple.

# Centering Prayer

Although the term *centering prayer* and its particular format came into being only within the past 40 years, the prayer is a summary of various silent prayer practices that can be traced back to the very beginnings of Christianity.[9] Again, you may find you've already engaged in such prayer without realizing it. This form of prayer trusts the direct and immediate availability of God, the "Indwelling Christ," who is nearer than our own heartbeat.

Centering prayer is a simplified form of contemplative prayer that draws on the latter steps of *lectio divina*. Because we live in a culture that increasingly lives in the "head"—ideas, calculations, abstractions, theologies—some people find *lectio divina* to be a particularly difficult form of contemplative prayer. For many of us in ministry, "thinking" about God often replaces "being" with God. When we read Scripture, we immediately begin to analyze the text, looking for interesting bits of meaning, lesson plans, or solutions to present day problems. This kind of study and analysis of the Bible is a critical and necessary part of ministry and Christian living, but it can be a hindrance—even a form of resistance—as we seek to be open and present to God.

allowing God to love us

---

[9] Forms of centering or silent prayer can be found in the writings of the early Desert Fathers and Mothers, Julian of Norwich, John of the Cross, and other mystical theologians and are most clearly articulated in the anonymously written fourteenth century devotional, *The Cloud of Unknowing*. One of the "founders" of centering prayer, M. Basil Pennington, sees centering prayer as a direct outgrowth of *lectio divina* in *Centering Prayer: Renewing an Ancient Christian Prayer Form.* For more on the history and tradition of centering prayer see "The Christian Contemplative Tradition and Centering Prayer," *Centering Prayer in Daily Life and Ministry,* Gustave Reininger, ed.

Imagine a woman sitting on the front porch at the end of the day, calling to her husband inside the house, and saying, "Work was so draining today. I couldn't wait to get home. Come sit next to me on the porch." The husband then comes to the doorway and replies, "Isn't it interesting how work takes up so much of our lives. I mean, here is this activity that we have to engage in to pay the bills; an activity that we hope will be satisfying at some level. Yet at the end of the day, we feel like we've been, as you say, 'drained.' Like something has been taken away from us or maybe we've given a part of ourselves that we now notice is missing. It's like we leave our true selves at work and..." For the next 30 minutes, the husband stands in the doorway sharing his reflections on the nature of work—all the while missing his wife's invitation to sit and be with her. We may find in *lectio* that we do the same. We spend most of our prayer time fascinated by our thoughts and reflections on the words we've read—and never really take time to sit and be with God.

In centering prayer we remove the temptation to spend our prayer time in thought and study. Again, it's not that biblical study and reflection is wrong; in fact, it's necessary to the Christian life. It's just that in contemplative prayer we seek to set aside our study and reflection in order to be fully attentive to God's presence.

Centering prayer is a direct, immediate, and deceptively simple form of silent prayer. The guidelines are as follows[10]:

- Sit comfortably in a space where you can open yourself to God. Have a set time to pray—10 minutes or so is good for starters. You may want to light a candle to help remind you of God's nearness.
- Before you begin the prayer, choose a sacred word as the symbol of your intention to be with God. This word expresses your desire to be in God's presence and to yield to the movement of the Holy Spirit. Ask the Holy Spirit to reveal a word that is suitable for you. Examples include *Jesus, Lord, Abba, Love,*

[10] These guidelines are modified from Thomas Keating's description of the Method of Centering Prayer found in many of his writings, including *Open Mind, Open Heart* and *Centering Prayer in Daily Life and Ministry.*

*Mercy, Stillness, Faith, Trust, Shalom,* and *Amen.* Once you've selected a word, stick with it. Occasionally people get caught up worrying whether their word feels right for them, wondering about the various meanings of their word, comparing their word to other words, or wondering if some other word might be more "spiritual" and produce "better" results. Don't take your word so seriously. It's simply a reminder of your desire to be with God. What's significant in this prayer is your intention (to be with God), and not your particular word.

- Before you pray, close your eyes and settle yourself. Allow a spirit of rest and hospitality to come over your body. Welcome God into this time. Briefly and silently introduce your sacred word as the symbol of your consent to God's presence and action within and around you. Thomas Keating suggests introducing the sacred word "inwardly and as gently as laying a feather on a piece of cotton."
- As you pray, you will become aware of thoughts, memories, commentaries, and images. When you notice your mind wandering, gently return to the sacred word. Thoughts are a normal part of centering prayer; yet by quietly returning to the sacred word, minimal effort is used to bring attention back to God.
- At the end of the prayer period, remain in silence with your eyes closed for a minute or two. You may want to close with the "Our Father" (Lord's Prayer) or some other formal prayer as a way of drawing the prayer to a close.

Centering prayer, like all forms of contemplative prayer, can be frustrating. Most of us have difficulty being present to another person, much less God. We might wish sometimes for a deity who is full of sights and sounds, one who would capture our attention in prayer with words and insight. Yet God often communicates in "sighs too deep for words" (Romans 8:26).

Often when I engage in centering prayer, I become overly aware of my chattering mind. I have long moments when I forget I'm praying, my attention lost in a thousand thoughts. I often find I don't get anything out of the prayer period itself; however, over time I have noticed dramatic shifts in my sense of God, my sense of self, and my commitment to following the way of Jesus. As a friend of mine once told me, in centering prayer "God is praying us." We wait with listening hearts while God speaks with words that only the deep recesses of our heart can perceive.

Whatever the form, the purpose of contemplative prayer is not that we might experience blissful moments of peace or escape the anxious reality of our lives. We practice contemplative prayer so we might become aware and receptive to the reality of life—even further, so we might become more in touch with God's presence in the middle of life, the Real within the real. We seek to make contact with God's love in the world—and coming into contact with love is not always peaceful. Like love itself, opening to the truth of God's presence can be painful, unearthing ignored questions and arousing nagging doubts. Moments of open, listening prayer not only help us become aware of God, but also may lead us to "sober up" to the truth of ourselves. Seeking to dwell within the Spirit of God, we often touch the truth of our situation. We notice our exhaustion, our frustration, our sin, our neediness, our latent hope. Often the fruit of contemplative prayer is not in the prayer itself but in the softening of the heart we experience in daily life. The Holy Spirit comforts and heals the deep wounds within us. Emotional knots are revealed or loosened. We yield to God's transforming work in ways that are difficult to perceive. Yet there are other moments when we notice, almost tangibly, God's Spirit moving and breathing within us.

As I've practiced contemplative prayer within youth ministry, I've noticed over time that situations with teenagers that used to provoke great stress and feelings of inadequacy or frustration now seem like just another part of the ministry. I sense a greater ability to act out of love and honesty with kids who are disruptive or challenging. I trust more in God's presence, and I'm less likely to lean entirely on my own efforts or charisma.

T.J. was a boy I found difficult to work with. He'd spent most of his teenage years being passed from one foster home to another. He was deeply wounded and needy for attention, yet possessed the energy of 10 chimpanzees. Every time T.J. showed up to a youth meeting, he would skateboard into the church building, crash into our classroom, and immediately begin talking at hyper-speed. Shifting back and forth in his seat, he would shout out a steady barrage of wisecracks at a volume usually reserved for punk rock clubs. I found myself irritated and reactive around T.J., and I felt relieved when he didn't show up.

I wanted to find a different way to relate to T.J., so I moved my prayer time with the other youth ministry leaders to a time just before our youth meeting. Although T.J. continued to be disruptive, gradually I noticed that my times of contemplative prayer were creating greater space and patience within me to work with T.J. I felt a growing sense of compassion for his situation, and even noticed that his attention-getting tactics weren't much different from my own. I still had difficulty working with T.J. and often had to set boundaries with him in order to facilitate the class. But as I spent each day surrendering myself and my ministry to God, I became more open to God's hope for T.J. and less attentive to my own issues and frustrations.

Contemplative prayer does not take away the anxiety or problems within ministry. There are still plenty of times when I take on too much responsibility with kids, plenty of moments when I react out of anger or anxiety. Yet these times of prayer help me notice when I am acting out of my own anxiety, pride, or neediness, rather than the truth and patience of God. Contemplative prayer has helped me mature in my faith and ministry and made me more aware of the true intentions behind my words and actions with kids.

allowing God to love us

As ministers it's important that we spend regular time in contemplative prayer. How can we share God if we don't spend time deepening our own relationship with God? Usually 10 minutes in the morning is a good start. Sometimes I find it helpful to begin my prayer time by dedicating it to the youth I serve. This reminds me that the prayer is not only for my benefit, but is deeply connected to the people I serve.

Young people are not looking for adults who have more poetic or more reasoned beliefs than they have. They're looking for adults who have experienced something, who trust something larger than themselves. They're looking for adults who "have heard with their own ears, seen with their own eyes, and touched with their own hands" (1 John 1:1). Our young people need us to spend regular periods of time yielding to God's life and love. They need us to be grounded in a Source of life larger than our own fretful concern. They need adults whose lives are "lit up," illumined by the awareness of God in the world.

In this culture we often feel guilty for taking time to rest. Downtime seems inefficient, unproductive, and useless. We tend to perceive ministry and the Christian life as a series of outward activities. We dismiss warnings from author and Episcopal priest Morton Kelsey that an efficiently busy life is "more potentially destructive of spiritual growth than debauchery or alcohol or hard drugs."

If we want young people to trust the mystery of God revealed in Jesus Christ, we need to inhabit the mysterious Being of God. We need to open to the spring of divine love from which our theologies, ethics, and doctrines grow. For if our words and actions are not watered by the healing love of God, our ministries will soon become dry and uninspired. Our hope is not simply to teach kids a set of beliefs. Belief is simply one step on the way to knowing God. Our hope is that our young people might know God and trust the way of life Jesus emblazoned—one in which a person lives in greater transparency to the reality of God and greater vulnerability to the presence of others. The theologies, ethics, and doctrines we seek to share with young people are meaningless unless they are enchanted by the sacred life of God.

If we are to minister to young people, then like Jesus we must set aside regular moments to stop, let go of our hold on life, and let God love us. This is Jesus' desire for us. This is the intention of contemplative prayer. This is the way our young people long for us to live.

# from prayer to presence

## 6

I continue to desire a more contemplative attitude toward youth ministry. I feel like it gives me license to just be present to our young people without feeling guilty about programming. I am able to sit and truly listen to them and revel in what they share about their lives. I find I enjoy the end of the evening, when the discussion is over and they hang out before being picked up by their parents. I get excited that they want to stay long enough to share what is going on in their lives. I think contemplative practice has helped me to see each of them as individuals and not as a collective group of "teenagers."

—LAWRENCE MOLLOY, YOUTH PASTOR, OUR LADY HELP OF CHRISTIANS, NEWTON, MASSACHUSETTS

Those who are unhappy have no need for anything in this world but people capable of giving them their attention. The capacity to give one's attention to a sufferer is a very rare and difficult thing; it is almost a miracle; it is a miracle.

—SIMONE WEIL, *WAITING FOR GOD*

contemplative youth ministry

The morning worship gathering at Westminster Presbyterian that day was unremarkable. The sanctuary was about two-thirds full with approximately 200 people, most topped with gray hair. I made my way up the aisle and took a seat in the front pew. After perusing the pastel worship bulletin, I looked up and was surprised to find 15 or 20 teenagers sitting to my immediate left in a makeshift set of benches. I later found out these "youth bleachers" were reserved as a special place for young people.

After the sermon a small group of church elders came forward to serve communion. The bread and wine was prayed over, the Spirit invoked, and a hymn sung. Congregants were then invited to come forward to share in the sacred elements. The orderly Presbyterians had a system. Starting with the back row, ushers directed people to rise and approach the communion table. As people filed forward, I noticed one of the communion assistants standing directly in front of me. She was an elderly woman, probably in her late 70s, gussied up the way elderly Presbyterian women often are with a silk jacket, white blouse, flowered skirt, and matching heels. She stood patiently, carefully steadying a heavy platter of bread. As people advanced she greeted them with a smile and in a quavering voice said, "This is the body of Christ, broken for you." There was a kindness and gentleness in her greeting, and I found myself gazing at her throughout the ritual.

Finally it was my turn to come forward. After taking the elements, I sat back down and returned my eyes to the elderly woman. I was startled by what I saw. Instead of the serene and gentle smile that had greeted me just a moment earlier, the woman's face was shuddering with emotion. With her head bowed and jaw knotted, she gripped the communion plate and struggled to keep her composure. I moved to the edge of the pew and prepared to step in when suddenly to the front of the sanctuary came the gangly group of teenagers. They rambled up in a whispering, giggling, nudging mob—causing another usher to spew numerous "shushes" while quickly sorting them into an orderly line. The young man at the front stepped forward and waited to receive the bread. I sat pensively, uncertain if I should offer help. The woman looked up, her eyes pouring tears, as she held the bread before the young man and said, "The body of Christ, broken for you, Thomas." The next young person approached. In a tender voice the elderly woman said, "The body of Christ, broken for you, Sarah." As the young people approached, she made an effort to look at each of them through her tears and slowly offered them the bread, while speaking their names with love.

At the end of the service, the associate pastor accompanied me to a meeting of the 15 adults who served in the youth ministry. I had asked to interview this group in order to learn about their efforts to incorporate contemplation in youth ministry. I sat down and looked across the circle of chairs and quickly noticed the elderly woman who had served communion. I introduced myself and discovered her name was Mildred. The meeting had yet to start, so I leaned forward and curiously prodded, "Mildred, you seemed to have a lot of emotion during communion this morning."

"Yes," she replied, smiling self-consciously. "It took me by surprise."

"I could see you have a lot of care for the young people," I prodded some more.

"Well, actually, most of those kids I've never met before." I gave her a quizzical look. "You see, I was asked to serve in the youth ministry by praying for the kids. I'm too old to run around with them, but I told Jen [the associate pastor] I could pray for them. Well, Jen took photos of all the kids and asked them to write their names on the back along with a prayer concern. All of us adults trade these pictures each week so that each of us gets time to pray for each kid. That was three years ago. Every morning, for three years, I have taken out my photos as part of my prayer time. I spend time just looking at the faces of those kids. Then I read their concerns and pray for them.

"This morning was the first time I've ever been asked to assist in communion. I felt so honored. And then suddenly I see these young faces coming toward me..." She welled up with tears and bowed her head for a few moments.

"I have beheld those faces for three years, praying for them and their futures. And then suddenly here they are in front of me, and I'm handing the bread of Christ to them. It was just too much, too overwhelming. I tried to stop each of them and just look at them and hug them with my eyes. I just felt so honored."

There is no greater gift we can give our youth than our full and loving attention. I often picture Mildred's face when I consider the way in which I seek to be present to young people in my own life. Notice that she felt honored to be with the youth—in the same way she felt honored to hold the bread of Christ. She was open and fully present, greeting each young person with a sense of gratitude and compassion. She was patient and slow, taking time to "behold" each young person. Her ability to receive those kids with love and compassion was directly connected to her times of prayer.

In my work with numerous youth ministry programs over the past 10 years, I've become convinced that the more we engage in contemplative, prayer the more we are able to be present to young people. In spending time beholding God, we learn to behold youth (and others). The transformation from anxiety to love takes place, I believe, as we learn to just "be" with God. Soon the attitude and presence we seek to embody in our relationship with God begins to permeate our relationships with young people. We develop a growing awareness of the presence of God within young people and notice that the patience we bring to contemplative prayer is also available

from prayer to presence

in our relationships with youth. *It's this movement from prayer to presence—from being open and available to God to being transparent and accessible before teens—that is the real work of ministry.*

It's easy to imagine a very different experience during my visit to Westminster Presbyterian. In most churches, you might expect that people would become flustered and irritated by the sight of a gangly group of teenagers swarming the communion table. In fact, five years earlier at that same church, youth and children were dismissed from the sanctuary before the worship service ever began. When the pastor demanded that the youth stay for at least the first half of the service, a large number of congregants became irate. It was only when the senior pastor threatened to quit that the elders of the church allowed youth to remain in the service. The transformation I witnessed within Mildred and other church members was dramatic. When I asked the staff and adult volunteers to account for the shift in how youth were perceived and treated in the congregation, they pointed to their times of individual and small group contemplative prayer dedicated to youth.

The conversion at Westminster did not go unnoticed by the youth. Not only were more of them attending the church, but more of them were also participating in worship, teaching in the Sunday school program, and serving in leadership positions. The welcome the youth experienced in the community of faith was very different from the receptions they got at school and in their neighborhoods. I remember meeting a 15 year-old boy named Nate who often came to worship on his own. When I asked him why, he told me:

> When I leave my house to go to church, I usually begin walking like I walk to school. But then as I come around my block and see the church building, I start smiling. And by the time I reach the curb in front of the church, I'm giggling. And then

when I reach the front door of the church, I'm just about ready to fall down laughing because I know as soon as I open that door all of these older folks are going to look over and see me and start smiling. Then they're going to come over and hug me and they're going to ask me all kinds of questions and they're going to want me to sit by them in the service. And that just cracks me up.

When I ran into Nate five years later, I was not surprised to hear he was working for a Christian organization that serves the rural poor. How could he resist participating in a community and a way of life that made him feel so valued?

If you look back over your own life, you may find that the moments that had the greatest impact on you were moments when you were in the presence of someone who was fully present to you. Give yourself the space, right now, to reflect on the last time you felt someone completely present and available to you. When was the last time you felt fully received by another person with compassion and care? What was it like?

Sadly, for many of us there are precious few moments among our many human interactions when we feel someone is fully present to us—even within our marriages and families. Most of us have so few experiences in which we have felt truly seen or listened to. Yet when those interactions do happen, they can be transformational. I'm convinced that many of us are Christians today because some person or group of people listened to us, saw us, received and delighted in us. This is the kind of presence our youth long for. This is the kind of presence Jesus embodied. This is the kind of presence we seek to incarnate in order to love young people into faith.

How do we offer this kind of presence to young people? How do we move from contemplative prayer to contemplative presence in our ministries with youth? The first step is noticing that contemplative awareness is something we're all familiar with. All of us have experienced moments of contemplative presence. All of us, like Mildred, have had moments of being fully present to another person. It's that full-hearted presence that comes over parents as they gaze upon their newborn baby. It's the quiet appreciation that descends on old friends as they sit together without speaking. It's neighbors sitting on the front porch, taking in the sights and sounds of the closing day. It's the elders from the temple sitting around 12 year-old Jesus, listening in wonder and amazement.

Even though it often goes unnoticed or unnamed, I believe contemplation is a common experience in the lives of Christians. It's the experience of being vulnerable to God in the present moment. It's an openness to reality, a gratitude for what is, a receptiveness to the Source of life. Thomas Merton refers to contemplation as "spiritual wonder," and suggests that it is, in some sense, the "experience" of Christian belief.[11] One thing is certain: contemplation is a grace. It's not an experience we can force or achieve. It's a gift when we discover we've been open and present to our lives and the life of God. Although we can't "make" ourselves contemplative, there are ways in which we can become more available to contemplation in our lives and in our relationships with youth.

[11] *New Seeds of Contemplation* (Plough Publishing, 1974), 5.

contemplative youth ministry

# being with young people

# 7

To listen tenderly and lovingly to the petty foibles, the painful longings, the relentless thirst for God that crowd into the consciousness of each of us is to listen, in fact, to God's own longing to live among and transform us. To listen to one another in this way is indeed to be a lover of souls.

—WENDY WRIGHT, "DESERT LISTENING,"
*WEAVINGS*, MAY-JUNE 1994

A contemplative approach to youth ministry has helped me see young people in a totally different way. I have "new eyes." I notice that as I give myself to stillness and contemplation, I see all things differently. I am able to hold them and "breathe them in." I believe I communicate to the kids by the way I am present to them—kids have told me that in times of need, it isn't what I say to them as much as the way in which I'm present to them. Previously, I was always thinking about what I was going to say to them; now I am able to simply be with them, listen, and then respond in faith.

—TAMMY CLARK, YOUTH PASTOR,
FIRST UNITED METHODIST CHURCH, VALPARAISO, INDIANA

contemplative youth ministry

As Christians, we want to move from prayer to presence, from receiving God in prayer to receiving God within our relationships with others. What does it mean to be present to the youth we serve? What would it look like to develop contemplative presence within our ministries?

My friend, Frank Rogers, from the Claremont School of Theology has laid out a description of being human that may best describe contemplative presence. He expresses it as "seeing and being seen, hearing and being heard, being moved by others and allowing others to be moved by us, responding with acts of kindness and receiving acts of kindness," and finally "embodying a sense of delight in all our interactions."[12] I want to utilize Rogers' categories of seeing, hearing, being moved to compassion, acting in kindness, and delighting, to help us get a sense of what it means to relate to youth from a place of love.

# Seeing

The Franciscan priest Richard Rohr writes that transformation in the spiritual life "is about seeing." It's about learning to see with the eyes of Jesus. As we bring contemplative awareness to our relationships with youth, we must first seek to simply see them. We love young people by seeing them as they are, not as the culture judges them to be or as we wish them to be. It's difficult for any of us to look at a young person (or any person for that matter) without judgment. It's difficult to receive young people just as they present themselves but without verbalizing or internalizing some sort of commentary. Often when we see a group of youth we immediately begin to assess them: "That freshman boy needs counseling, that one dresses too provocatively, that girl must have rich parents..." *labeling*

Seeing is our first language. For most of us, it's the way we first make contact with the world. My daughter, Grace, is 16 months old.

[12] Frank Rogers, "Perichoretic Personhood: The Dancing Movement of Love" (Religion and Psychotherapy Conference. Institute for Religion, Texas Medical Center, Houston, TX, October 1994).

being with young people

If you were here with me and she came into the room, she would look at you a long time. Her eyes would be clear, open, and vulnerable. She would examine your facial expression, take note of your body posture, and closely watch your reactions to her. When Grace sees people, she *sees* them. She receives them through her eyes. All of us understand this way of seeing; all of us have looked with Grace's eyes. It's these same open eyes that we seek to inhabit when we encounter youth.

As I read the New Testament, it's clear to me that people felt seen by Jesus. It's also clear that Jesus' willingness to openly see people (particularly those who often went unseen and unnoticed) was at the heart of his ministry. When Jesus enters the town of Nain, he is accompanied by a large crowd. You can imagine the activity, conversation, and sense of excitement that surrounded him. As the teacher and his followers enter the town, they encounter a funeral procession. A young man has died and his body is being carried outside the city gates, closely followed by his grieving, widowed mother and a large crowd of mourners. Luke writes, "When the Lord saw her, he had compassion for her" (Luke 7:13).

Jesus sees the woman. He takes in the woman through his eyes. He sees and receives her grief. Out of this seeing arises compassion and later a healing act. But it is the seeing that comes first. Later in Luke's Gospel, Jesus tells the story of the prodigal son, and the same movements are repeated. The younger son walks up the road to his father's house confused, hungry, and downcast. The passage reads, "But while he was still far off, his father saw him and was filled with compassion; he ran, put his arms around him and kissed him" (Luke 15:20). The father sees his son and notices his dejected posture. Compassion arises and he responds with an act of reconciliation.

When we seek to be contemplatively present to young people, we seek to see them through the eyes of love. We look at them the way we might look at our loved ones when they sleep. It's such a sweet pleasure to gaze upon someone as they sleep. It's a time of beholding them, of setting aside words and roles and allowing your eyes to rest upon them, taking in and enjoying who they are. I remember traveling with a particularly difficult group of teens to do a summer service project. We stopped to sleep in a church for the night and, after unloading the vans, the kids went berserk. They were racing down the aisles of the sanctuary with wheelchairs, putting on choir robes, hiding in the pipe organ, and climbing over the pews. I became angry and shouted biting remarks at them. I demanded that they get into their sleeping bags, turned out the lights, and told them to go to sleep immediately.

An hour later I was still agitated and irritable and couldn't sleep. I felt badly about how I had treated the youth. I got up and walked around the sanctuary. Kids were sleeping in pews, in the aisle, and next to the altar. I walked among them and knelt down to gaze at several of them as they slept. I noticed their innocence. I remembered the pain many of these kids carried—several of them were foster kids, abandoned by their parents. I suddenly felt compassion for them. They were excited to be on a trip, to get away from their families, to travel with their friends. I had been so aware of my own fatigue and my concern about messing up the church building that I hadn't seen how eager the kids were to play and run and release the energy pent up from a day of sitting on a bus. I realized I could have been more aware of their need to move and more straightforward in asking them to respect the church property.

That night I sat and simply looked at each young person, seeking to see each face through Jesus' eyes. When we gathered the next morning to begin the day with prayer, I apologized for my outburst. I allowed the group to see my own frustration and struggle as a youth leader. I told them that, although I needed to remind them to care for the church building, I didn't need to yell at them with such anger. I was surprised to see lots of forgiving smiles around the group. Then one young person responded, "I've never heard an adult apologize before." Then another spoke up: "I guess we owe you an apology as well. You were tired from driving all day and probably were worried about being responsible for the building. Sorry we weren't more careful."

When was the last time you looked at young people openly, without judgment or expectation? When was the last time you tried to look at someone with the eyes of God? When was the last time a young person felt seen by you? When was the last time you allowed a young person to see you as you really are? Can we look at young people with soft eyes? Can a young person come into our churches or ministries and really be seen? Who might our young people become if every Christian they encounter beholds them with eyes of love?

## , Hearing

To be contemplatively present to young people also means to listen. It means opening our ears to the words and feelings youth speak. In the church we like talking; in fact, it may be our primary practice. We forget that the majority of Jesus' teaching came after listening to the request or question of another person. As ministers we feel it's our job to talk. Often our whole youth program—our activities, music, snacks, and outings—is all designed to help kids sit and listen to us talk. We rarely turn it around and create programs designed to help us listen to young people. Yet I'll bet you can recall very few words from the countless sermons, lectures, speeches, and conversations you've heard in your life. In contrast, I would wager you remember most of the moments when you felt deeply listened to and heard by another person. It's almost a conversion experience in this day and age to be authentically heard by another person. So many of us don't really listen to others—instead we nod our heads, waiting for our turn to speak. Or when we do listen, we listen with an agenda, a filter. We listen for "the right answer." We listen to see if they can repeat what we've told them. Too often we ignore or become uninterested in the words of young people when they don't fit our lesson plan.

What would it be like for us to listen to youth openly, without preparing our response? What would it be like for youth to truly be heard within our churches and communities of faith? What if we trusted the advice of St. Francis, who told his followers to "preach the gospel, and if necessary, use words"?

I once led an exercise with a group of teenagers in which I asked them to remember a time when they felt deeply heard. Then I asked each person to share a word that captured how it felt. I wrote down their words:

Relief

Affirmed

Held

Cared for

Loved

Relevant

Freed up

Overwhelmed

Eternal

Expanded

Humbled

Important

Like God was present

Imagine if you were heard—and deeply listened to—in every relationship. Who would you become? Take a moment to remember an experience when you felt heard, a moment in which someone listened to you openly, without an agenda? What was that like?

Recently a group of teenagers from a rough, poverty-stricken area of San Francisco were asked to write essays about peace. The project was funded as a response to the terrorist attack on the World Trade Center. Instead of writing about peace, the youth ended up writing about violence—it turned out this was much closer to their experience. When the essays were finished, the publisher asked the youth to come up with a title for the book. They decided to call it *Waiting to Be Heard*. This phrase comes to me often when I encounter young people: *waiting to be heard*. If we seek to share the presence of Christ with young people, we need to let go of all our words, admonishments, and advice, and simply be with young people and listen to them. Listen to them in the same way we yearn to be listened to. Listen to them with the patient ears of Jesus. Dietrich Bonhoeffer summarizes the importance of ministry through listening:

> The first service that one owes to others in the fellowship consists in listening to them. Just as love to God begins with listening to His Word, so the beginning of love for our brothers and sisters is learning to listen to them...Christians, especially ministers, so often think they must always contribute something when they are in the company of others. They forget that listening can be a greater service than speaking. Many people are looking for an ear that will listen. They do not find

it among Christians, because these Christians are talking where they should be listening. But the person who can no longer listen to others will soon be no longer listening to God either...This is the beginning of the death of the spiritual life, and in the end there is nothing left but spiritual chatter and clerical condescension arrayed in pious works...Christians have forgotten that the ministry of listening has been committed to them by the One who is the great listener and whose work they should share. We should listen with the ears of God that we may speak the Word of God."[13]

# Moved to Compassion

When we take the time to see and hear young people, often we find compassion rising within us. When we see with the eyes of Jesus and hear with the ears of Jesus, we soon find ourselves feeling with the heart of Jesus. Many adolescents are faced with the task of recruiting people who care for them. Young people move outside their family circles, looking for friends, mentors, and communities who will take an interest in them. Tragically, few young people are able to attract adults and communities who have the interest or time to spend with them.

When we seek to be present to young people, we let down the walls of our heart and allow ourselves to be moved by them. As youth ministers, we seek to have soft hearts—hearts that can be touched by the joy, confusion, loneliness, anger, or tears of young people.

[13] Excerpts from "The Ministry of Listening" in *Life Together*, trans. John Dobbenstein (New York: Harper & Row, 1954), 97-99.

being with young people

It's hard for those of us who minister with young people to feel the struggle of being young. It's easy for us to trivialize the pain and experience of youth. Yet we know that our lives are still marked by many of the pains and joys of our own adolescence. Can we allow ourselves to be moved by the young people in our lives?

Can we stop and take the time to feel life from their perspective?

The most profound example of the power of open-hearted presence I've ever witnessed occurred while I was leading a high school youth group. I was conducting a discussion on the difficulty of talking about our faith with people outside the church. To help stimulate the discussion, we set up a role play. The scene was simple: a high school cafeteria. One person, hostile to Christianity, was having lunch next to another young person who was reading a Christian devotional. I placed a table and two chairs at the front of the room and then asked for volunteers to play the two roles and allow the conversation to be a sort of spontaneous drama.

Immediately Daniel stood up and took the seat of the person hostile to the faith. Then Sarah walked up and took the seat of the Christian young person who was reading a devotional. We started the drama, and soon Daniel was ridiculing Sarah for her faith, claiming Christianity was a psychological crutch. Sarah, playing the role of the devout Christian, did her best to explain that the faith is more than just psychological comfort, but Daniel was persistent. Soon Sarah became flustered and, in line with the rules of the role play, raised her hand and asked for someone to take her place.

Julie, a freshman, stepped up and began defending the Christian faith using different Bible verses to back her claims. Daniel, however, was ruthless: "The Bible was made up just like all myths are made up. How can you believe in a God you've never seen? How can you claim this God is good when there is so much suffering in the world?" His emotion was so vivid, it became clear that Daniel was no longer doing a role play. His anger and questions were his own. I became worried that the exercise was getting out of hand, but I didn't know how to close it gracefully.

Julie raised her hand, and Sam came up and tried to respond to Daniel's questions. Daniel grew even more upset, setting aside all pretense of the role play, and unloaded: "Listen, I was born in South Central—one of the roughest parts of Los Angeles. When I was four years old, my best friend and I were walking to the park when a gun fight broke out. We stood frozen—just watching these gang kids shooting at each other. My friend Benjamin got hit in the chest by a stray bullet. I sat there screaming and crying and watched him die. Now you tell me God is good and loving! What kind of God allows a four-year-old kid to die like that?"

The room became starkly quiet. None of us knew how to respond. Sam quietly raised his hand. For a moment everyone stayed still. Then Jake stood up and said, "I'll take Sam's place." Jake was the last guy I'd have chosen to respond to Daniel's outburst. Five months earlier Jake had been arrested for burglarizing houses for drug money. His sentence was to attend an outdoor rehabilitation program deep in the mountains of Idaho where, after living with other youth offenders in plastic tarp tents, he was sent out alone to spend a week in the wilderness to survive by his own wits. Jake was a big, strong kid who had attended church to get away from his parents, and he'd shown little interest in the Christian faith. I was worried he would take this opportunity to join Daniel in creating a scene and ridiculing Christianity. But for some reason, I didn't stop him from heading to the front of the room.

After walking up to the makeshift stage, Jake removed the table, turned his chair, and sat facing Daniel with open, steady eyes. There was a minute or so of silence as Jake continued to sit, relaxed and patient, just gazing at Daniel. Many of us felt awkward, and I stood there, unsure whether I should interrupt. Finally, Daniel spoke up and began to accost Jake, "So what do you have to say? That my friend Benjamin went to a better place? That this was part of God's plan? That God makes us suffer so we'll turn to him? How can you possibly believe all this crap about God being a God of love?"

Jake just sat there. I assumed he was planning a response, when gradually Daniel quieted, sat still, and returned Jake's gaze. And then something broke. Daniel's hard expression softened, his eyes searched Jake's, and then I noticed what he was looking at. There were tears on Jake's face. Quietly, without looking away from Daniel, Jake let tears fall down his face. Daniel gazed at Jake in wonder for a moment, then his eyes swelled with tears, and he lowered his head. Slowly, Jake stood up, raised Daniel from his chair, and hugged him. After a few minutes they both stepped down and returned to the group. Jake never spoke a word.

The whole group sat stunned, unsure of what they had just seen. I encouraged the group to sit in silence for a moment, offered a short prayer, and dismissed the class. Two weeks later, Daniel began showing up to church—not just for youth activities, but for morning worship. He came to Bible studies and served on the leadership team for the youth ministry. I never asked him about that night when Jake felt his tears, but I'm convinced that Jake was the presence of Christ to Daniel. His willingness to see, hear, and feel Daniel's pain was the good news that Daniel longed to encounter.

When was the last time you were moved by a young person's situation? When was the last time you felt joy or pain in empathy with a young person? Youth ministers strive to be people who are easily moved by the experiences of adolescents—their joy as well as their suffering. We have hearts that savor the energy, questions, and struggles of young people. Like Jesus, we find that through seeing, hearing and being with kids, we cultivate an open-hearted compassion for young people. With every young person we encounter, we find compassion rising up within us the way it did for the father when he noticed his lost son walking up the road; the way it did for the Samaritan when he looked upon the traveler, beaten and hurting at the side of the road; the way it did for Jesus, who saw the eager faces of the children, turned to the disciples, and said, "Let the little children come to me, do not stop them" (Mark 10:14).

# Act with Kindness

When we allow ourselves to be moved by the experience of young people, it's only natural to respond with acts of kindness. Just as the Good Samaritan sees the man in the ditch, feels compassion, and works to help the poor traveler, we too are invited to engage in ordinary actions that foster healing and encouragement.

Acts of kindness are moments in which we embody the love of God. Our kindness toward young people is a way of blessing them, a way of caring for them and letting them know they are valued. Kindness often takes place in small, hidden acts. We see these small acts of kindness in Jesus: making wine for a wedding party, giving bread and fish to a hungry crowd, cleaning the feet of the disciples, preparing breakfast on the beach for his friends. The love of God is often more powerful and transformative in these small acts of love than in the lights, energy, and charisma of large outreach events. What if we became more aware of the small ways in which we engage young people? What if our ministry was about giving rides home, sharing snacks, opening doors, helping carry book bags, and giving compliments when a young person has taken great care in his appearance? These small acts of kindness are little blessings, balms that heal the many mean and belittling messages young people receive each day.

As Christians we've always known we're expected to act with kindness toward others. But when our deeds of charity come from a greater sense of God's presence, we're able to bring our whole selves to the task. We're able to engage in these acts of love with a greater sense of Jesus' companionship. They become not just moments of service, but moments when we are being expanded and nurtured by God. We become aware, as Jesus suggests, that in these acts of love we're not just carrying a book bag for a young person, we're also making contact with Jesus. We begin to feel more and more that we're participating in God's mission of love, rather than serving some moral ideal.

At one church where I served as volunteer youth minister, church members would provide a Sunday dinner for the youth. There was always salad, a main course, dessert, and drinks. Each Sunday the other youth ministry volunteers and I would carefully set up the tables, lay out the silverware, and arrange the food in preparation for the meal. As the youth arrived, we were intentional about greeting all of them by name, often giving them big hugs and then inviting them to sit at the table. The meals would last up to an hour and were filled with conversation and laughter. Many kids told us it was the only "real food" (as opposed to fast-food or microwave dinners) they received all week.

After dinner we'd play games, sing, pray, and engage in Bible study. But as I look back on my time at that church, I'm convinced the care we put into greeting kids and serving them dinner was probably our most effective communication of the Christian life. Those dinners were filled with small acts of kindness and care directed toward the young people each week. If I interviewed the kids who came through that ministry over the five years I served there, I'll bet they wouldn't remember many lessons we taught, but I'm sure they would remember our times of eating, talking, and laughing together around a table prepared with love and care.

When we take the time to be present and open to youth, we find our actions are less frenetic, less about meeting some outside expectation, and less about us. Instead, our emphasis is on doing what's needed and responding in love to the situation before us. I witnessed a powerful example of such kindness several years ago while I was

Christmas shopping. Despite my intention to keep the celebration of Jesus' birth restful and relational, I found myself rushing through a mall three days before Christmas, frantically searching for something for my wife. Having successfully located the perfect gift, I sat in the food court of the mall, wolfing down Chinese food. Suddenly, into the cluster of brightly lit food stalls came 10 developmentally disabled folks accompanied by two assistants with sweatshirts that read, "The Redwoods Group Home." In contrast to the other hustling and harried shoppers, these folks lumbered, almost otherworldly, through the tables and crowds, smiling and sometimes clapping hands or yelling with genuine pleasure at the sights and smells of the eating arena.

With slow and careful effort, the assistants helped each person decide what food to purchase, stand in line, order a meal, pay for the meal, and carry the food back to a table. The assistants spent much of the time conversing and sharing in the excitement of the disabled folks who were ecstatic about the personal sovereignty they were afforded amidst so many tasty delights. The assistants patiently helped people get their food and get seated before serving themselves. There was one man with Down Syndrome, however, who shook off every offer of aid by the assistants. He knew what he wanted, and he wanted to do it himself. The assistants acquiesced and, watching from a safe distance, let him walk to the McDonald's booth and stand in line. The young man stood with import and dignity holding a red-and-yellow coupon in his hand. When he reached the front of the line, he handed the paper over to the cashier, spoke loudly, and gestured toward a stack of various cups and the coffee machine. The cashier obliged, and a few moments later the young man returned to his friends holding a giant 32-ounce cup of coffee, his face beaming with pride.

I stood up to hit one last store before going home. After my final purchase, I stepped through two smoky glass doors into the parking lot and found myself behind the folks from the group home. Rain was coming down in buckets, and the assistants had their charges staying dry under the eaves of the mall entrance. One by one the assistants accompanied the members of the group across the slippery sidewalk into a waiting van. Back and forth the assistants went, their clothes weighed down with water as they sought to keep the young people dry. As I stepped around the group, I noticed the young man with the McDonald's coffee. He was bent over his hard-earned brew, sheltering it from the downpour. Then without any apparent direction from the assistants, he took off from the side of the building, spontaneously bolting for the warmth and security of the van. But he stopped halfway across the sidewalk, startled by the heavy rain, and turned to return to the cover of the mall eaves. One of the assistants saw him turn back and yelled to him to continue his route toward the vehicle. Increasingly shocked and confused by the soaking water, he twisted his body toward the voice of the assistant with a quick jerk that caused the 32-ounce coffee cup to slip from his hands and break open against the wet concrete. Across the gray sidewalk, the caffeine flowed like a mud slide. The young man froze, took in the sight of his lost purchase, and began to cry. Soon his body gave way, and he slumped down into the steaming puddle. It was a pitiful sight to see this young man wailing mournfully, sitting in a growing pond of coffee, the dark rain soaking his clothes.

We all looked on in helpless sympathy when one of the assistants, a 20 something woman, stepped out of the van. She ran over to the young man, sat down in the cold wet coffee, wrapped her arm around him, placed his head on her shoulder, and let him cry. For several minutes she sat there with the patience of God, just holding the young man while rain poured down. I stood transfixed, somehow aware that I was gazing upon one of the deep spiritual truths of our relationships with one another, of our capacity to care for one another, of the way in which we participate in the power of God's healing love through gentle acts of solidarity and kindness. When the man had calmed, the young assistant took his hand, lifted him from the concrete, and led him to the front passenger seat of the van. She helped him with his seat belt, gave him a kiss, and shut the door. Her clothes slung with water, her jeans stained brown, she stepped into the van, slid the door shut, and then squeezed her body into the backseat.

The assistant from the Redwoods Group Home wasn't responding according to some prescribed method of behavior. She wasn't following a program or curriculum in her actions toward the young man. Her response was natural, flowing from her willingness to be present to the people she served. She chose to sit in the teeming rain because she saw the young man, heard his cry, and felt her heart go out to him. All of the assistants had responded to the needs of the disabled people with a series of small acts of kindness—from helping people get their food, to finding chairs and tables, to walking folks through the rain, to giving a troubled person the best seat on the van. This is the same way in which we seek to respond to young people—with actions that flow from relationship, from attentiveness, from compassion, and from transparency to God's love.

Contemplation isn't just being still. As Parker Palmer once wrote, "At root, contemplation and action are the same."[14] As our youth ministry becomes infused with contemplative prayer and awareness, the effect is not more prayer and silence; instead, what begins to emerge is authentic action. Activities within the youth ministry no longer are chosen frantically from resource books; they no longer are prescribed from the outside. Instead, as we widen our awareness, our actions with youth become more guided by their needs and the movement of the Holy Spirit. Being prayerfully present to kids enlarges our capacity to act out of love rather than anxiety. Contemplative awareness nurtures our creativity and draws us to act from the heart. We find ourselves responding more and reacting less.

Think about the last time you received an act of kindness. What was the experience like? How often do youth experience kindness within your community of faith? What would your relationship and

being with young people

[14] *The Active Life* ( HarperSanFrancisco, 1991).

ministry with young people be like if you attended to the small actions that reveal the kindness of Jesus?

## Delight

Jesus spent most of his life in wonder. He stood in wonder at the beauty of the natural world, the pain and suffering of people, and the faith of strangers. He stood in wonder at the little ones—the marginalized and discarded children. He stood amazed at the willingness of people to repent and participate in God's work in the world. He stood enchanted by God's love and devotion to humanity.

One sign that we're called to serve youth is that we are easily amazed and delighted by them. As ministers, we not only take the time to see, hear, and be moved by their experiences, we also infuse every interaction with a sense of delight. People who hope to share the Christian faith with teenagers are people who delight in young people. Within each interaction we seek to get a glimpse of their beauty, their gifts, and their belovedness in God.

There may be nothing more pleasurable, more nurturing, and more healing than being in the presence of someone who genuinely delights in you. I see this in my children. They want me to watch them do a back-flip off the couch, to look at a drawing of a boat, to eat the cookie. They call my attention to themselves over and over each day. What they seek is not pointers on gymnastic form or comparisons with other visual artists or comments on the texture of the cookie. What they want is for me to yell, "Wow! What a flip!" They want me to look at their drawings and say, "I love the way you drew that mast, and look here at the anchor—that looks so real!" They long for me to taste their new cookie creation, close my eyes, and say, "This is incredible! I could eat 20 of these!" What my kids want—what we all want—is delight. They want to feel that their presence, their gifts, their expressions, and their yearnings are a source of joy in the world.

This is the spirit of contemplative presence. When I seek to be prayerfully open and available to young people, I seek to see each individual. To hear her joys. To be moved by his experiences. To respond with kindness. And then, in all my interactions I seek to embody a sense of delight in each young person's presence in the world—even in the midst of suffering or great brokenness. This is what it means to love like Jesus. This is the good news Jesus calls us to share.

Jean Vanier once wrote that love is "to reveal the beauty of another person to themselves."[15] This is why we seek to be fully present to young people. Because when youth are seen, they feel valued. When they are heard, they feel respected. When someone is moved by their situation, they feel loved. When they receive kindness, they feel cared for. And when others delight in their existence, they sense the very breath of God.

Youth ministry is about holding a young person's deepest identity until he or she is able to see it too. We hold onto the knowledge that these young people are the beloved of God, that they have gifts that enrich the world, and that their presence is a cause for celebration. We hold this understanding of young people until they can hold it for themselves. We seek to reveal their beauty back to them until they see it, until they believe it, until they can live from it grounded in God's love.

What would it mean if the goal of our ministries was simply to be prayerfully present to young people—to allow them to be fully themselves? Could we trust that our presence is enough? How would we treat youth if we weren't trying to convince them of the importance of the faith, the worthiness of Jesus, the necessity of the church? What would happen if we sought to minister to young people through our

[15] Jean Vanier, founder of l'Arche, a faith-based international network of more than 100 communities in 30 countries for people with disabilities. *Becoming Human* (Paulist Press, 1999), 22.

being with young people

ears, through our presence, through silent prayer and an open heart? What would such radical acceptance evoke in young people?

Contemplative youth ministry is about deepening our presence to both God and young people. Although contemplative ministry is grounded in prayer and openness to God, the fruit of this time is our increasing ability to be present—open and available—in all our relationships. Taking time to engage in contemplative prayer prepares us for wonder and amazement. When we slow down we are able to see the miracle of living life and the power of God's presence in the world. Like Jesus, we let go of any attempts to manipulate or pressure young people into the faith, and instead trust the slow work of God.

# remembering

**8**

My dedication to the youth in my midst has deepened, and they have become not a responsibility but a gift and a treasure in my life in a new way. When I listen to them, I listen to them. Because I am listening more, I care more, and because I care more, they talk more. Contemplative practice has changed my paradigm about God and so I am a better model for the youth I encounter. I have learned that God is also within me, that I am beloved, that I can do all things with God, and that Love always wins, always. How can that not impact the youth I'm with? I am able to be present for JT who has been in foster homes while his mother was recovering from alcohol abuse. JT knows he is beloved and that I care. I am able to be present to JT because I am centered with God. When I am with him, I am not thinking about 10 other things I could/should/ought to be doing next.

—LAURIE RODNEY, EDUCATIONAL CONSULTANT, PARENT AND YOUTH MINISTRY VOLUNTEER, CHURCH OF THE REDEEMER, CLEVELAND, OHIO

The lightest and most ordinary encounter with the laughing God happens in the little instant of remembering love after we have been forgetful. For me it is one of the most precious experiences of living: to have been kidnapped by some worry or striving and then suddenly to be gracefully returned home to the present moment and reminded of love. It is almost always an occasion for the giggles.

GERALD MAY, *THE AWAKENED HEART*

contemplative youth ministry

Young people have no presumptions about receiving anyone's full attention. They're formed in a world that expects and rewards distraction. They assume when the phone rings that the caller is simultaneously driving a car, playing a video game, or standing at a cash register. They're trained to believe that successful people are the ones who can divide their attention among the largest number of activities. To be seen, heard, and fully attended to by another is wishful thinking. People are too busy. Life is too hectic. There are too many tasks to be accomplished, goals to be achieved, and diversions to be experienced.

And we have to admit that being present to a young person—or any person, for that matter—is incredibly difficult. We too have been shaped by a society that demands multitasking. We too grew up doing homework in front of chattering television sets and blaring stereos. We too have been trained to lift up efficiency, instead of relationship, as the highest value in ministry. Furthermore, many of us who work with teenagers have been successful because we're so good at multitasking! We're people with high energy who can make arrangements for a ski retreat and plan a Bible study all while driving to pick up pizza for Sunday school class. No one expects us to be fully present to kids, least of all the church. We continually receive the message that parents, church board members, and pastors are happy as long as we produce as many programs in as few hours as possible. I've counseled and talked with many youth directors and church volunteers who've been let go from their youth ministry responsibilities. None of them were dismissed for not being present to kids. Most were let go because they weren't increasing the number of kids and programs within the church.

In a society that increasingly seeks to fracture our attention, contemplative presence becomes an act of rebellion. It's a radical in-breaking of the Holy Spirit every time we seek to be prayerfully present to another human being. However, just as we must continually return again and again to contemplative prayer in order to keep our hearts open and attentive to the presence of God, so too must we intentionally cultivate contemplative presence with young people.

Being contemplatively present to young people is often a matter of forgetting and remembering. Over and over, I forget that the souls of young people are not in my hands. I have to remember that I'm not the center of the world. I forget that young people are more in need of my presence than my knowledge. I have to remember that my presence and trust in God is enough. Jesus knew that forgetting is a serious problem for those who seek to live the Christian life. His last words, as recorded in the book of Matthew are, "Remember, I am with you always, to the end of the age" (Matthew 28:20).

*Being present to God amidst young people and being present to young people amidst God takes practice.* It takes practice to remember you're not alone. It takes practice to remember that God is present and available within our relationships with kids. It takes practice to receive young people with the eyes, ears, and heart of Jesus. In this chapter you will find exercises and practices I've used to help me remember God's nearness and my desire to be open and receptive to young people.

# The Only Jesus You'll Ever Know

My first son, Noah, was born while I was a graduate student in seminary. I was working on a master's degree in Christian spirituality and spent most days listening to lectures and most nights absorbed in reading great mystical texts. Soon after Noah was born, I took him to a seminary chapel service. After the service ended, I encountered one of my mentors, Sister Elizabeth Liebert, who serves as the Professor of Spiritual Life at San Francisco Theological Seminary. She is a wise and prayerful teacher, and a primary reason I decided to study Christian spirituality. Beth was elated to see my new son. I let her hold him, and she gazed in delight at his face, commenting on his dark eyes and little bow mouth. She placed her finger on his head and made the sign of the cross, blessed him, and then handed him back to me and said, "This is your greatest teacher, Mark. Treat him as such." She looked at me while her words sunk in and then walked off.

As these words took hold, I found myself looking at Noah with new eyes. This little helpless child who depended on his mother and me for care was my greatest teacher. I began to gaze on Noah with a new sense of expectation. Instead of attending to him as a series of needs that required attention, I began to be more open and receptive. I would watch him, wondering what gift he was seeking to give me, what insight he might offer, what "lesson" this teacher sought to impart. I began to see my time with Noah as sacred. During the night hours, I would wake up to his cry and think of the monks at the local monastery where I spent retreats. They too were waking throughout the night to sing and pray and attend to the presence of Christ. Over time these midnight walks with Noah became times of prayer, times of receiving God's love and insight. I tried to attend to Noah as if I were holding the baby Jesus himself, in wonder and anticipation.

When I began training to become a youth minister, there was a phrase commonly used in books and workshops to highlight the importance of our behavior toward youth: "You may be the only Jesus they'll ever know." This statement was intended to emphasize how important it is for youth workers to pay special attention to their behavior toward and among young people because they are representing Christ to those teenagers. I agree that we ministers need to be reminded that we seek to embody the same spirit of love and hospitality that Jesus embodied. As followers of Jesus we seek to have the "mind of Christ" and to disclose God's life in the world just as Jesus did. However, this idea of "being Jesus" for the young people in our lives can warp our relationships by putting too much emphasis on us. When we seek to *be* Jesus, we become the center of attention. We're the ones who act, teach, heal, and lead. As "Jesus," we can't help but feel like the spotlight is on us. This creates undue pressure and can actually keep us from embodying the kind of patience and generosity of spirit Jesus embodied.

Over the years I've found it much more helpful to follow the advice of Sister Liebert and seek to treat each young person as a teacher from God, someone God has placed in my life in order to help me grow in faith. When I encounter a young person, I find it much more helpful to think that she (or he) may be the only Jesus I'll ever know. Perhaps by seeking to encounter the presence of Christ in young people, we'll find ourselves better able to see them, hear them, feel compassion for them, and respond in kindness. Certainly Jesus encouraged us to see and treat others in this way. In the Gospel of Matthew, Jesus says God's kingdom will be inherited by those who brought him food when he was hungry and drink when he was thirsty, who clothed him when he was naked, who cared for him when he was sick, and who visited him while he was imprisoned. When the righteous can't remember when they did those things for Jesus, he tells them, "Truly I tell you, just as you did it to one of the least of these who are members of my family, you did it to me" (Matthew 25:40).

Jesus does not align himself with the givers of care, he identifies with "the least of these." That's where his presence is to be found. Before your next encounter with young people, pause for a few minutes and pray that God will help you receive your young people as if each of them were Jesus. Close your eyes and picture their faces; ask God to remind you that each of these young people was created in the image of God. Then as you're with the teenagers, see if you can receive them in the same way the elders of the Jewish temple received young Jesus. See if you can listen to and visit with them in wonder and amazement.

Like Jesus, young people can fill us with doubt and questions. Like Jesus, they can unearth broken and unfinished places within us. Like

Jesus, they can bring us to the edge of our capacities to love and forgive...and then demand more. Can we see that maybe the reason God has drawn us into youth ministry isn't because we have something to offer, but because there is something we need to receive? Maybe God gathers those 13-year-olds into your Sunday school classroom because it's the only place where God can get your attention. Perhaps you are more pliable among these youth, more open to God shaking you up or offering you a word of healing. Maybe youth ministry is your spiritual discipline. It's not just a place where you serve, it's a place where you're transformed, healed, and made new. Can you see it that way? Try interacting with young people as if they are instrumental to your own freedom and healing.

# The Interior Glance

Another way to remember God's constant presence within our interactions with young people is to practice the "interior glance" of Brother Lawrence. A Carmelite lay-brother, Brother Lawrence was not a scholar, teacher, or skilled worker in his community. He spent most of his days working in the kitchen—and even there he proved to be clumsy and at times quite incompetent. But Brother Lawrence was a person who knew how to love well. He knew how to live in deep communion with God and with great compassion for others. He's remembered to this day for the simple way in which he dwelt within the presence of God and showered care on those he encountered. He found a way to illuminate the mundane activities of life with an abiding awareness of God's nearness that he called "practicing the presence of God."

One of the ways Brother Lawrence achieved a sense of God's presence in his normal activities was by simply glancing "God-ward" throughout the day. These interior glances came as unplanned, unforced moments when he would remember God's presence and simply turn his heart's attention to God, opening to God in the midst of doing dishes, cleaning floors, or conversing with others.

I have three children who are often with me when I'm in public places or out running errands. Sometimes when I'm grocery shopping or chatting with a friend, my kids will wander off. But no matter how engaged I am in an activity or conversation, I still have an ongoing awareness of the presence of my children. There's this sixth sense that attends to them, listens for them, notices when they're in need. Even when I'm deeply engaged in conversation, my head will turn suddenly (before I even know why) just before one of my kids jumps off a shopping cart or pulls down a carton of eggs. As a parent I know the experience of practicing the presence of my children while engaged in other activities. In a similar way we can attend to the presence of God while relating to young people. We seek to keep the heart's eye on God, noticing God's expansive presence in all of our interactions with youth.

There are different ways we can remind ourselves to look toward God during our encounters with youth. First of all, we can pray, asking God to remind us of God. This is a helpful prayer to say before we encounter young people. Whether they are returning home from school, waiting in a church classroom, or walking toward us on a sidewalk, we can take a moment to breathe a simple prayer asking God to remind us of God's presence as we relate to young people.

Brother Lawrence took advantage of the little spaces within a day to remind himself of God's abiding love. We can do the same. No matter how busy we are, there are always little pauses, spaces within our daily routine that we can use as reminders to pray and notice God. I've found that these spaces exist even within a busy youth event or church class. There are still little breaks during which I can take a breath and turn my attention toward God—sitting alone in the youth room waiting for the kids to arrive, walking to the kitchen to get snacks for Sunday school, during the few seconds of silence before the kids begin the closing prayer, waiting in my car to give a young person a ride to school. There are many moments in our interactions with young people that we can use to intentionally remind ourselves to stop and receive the Holy Spirit.

I've also used images and sounds as reminders to glance Godward. For eight years I lived next to a seminary that sounded chapel bells every hour. Every time I noticed the sound of the bells, I would simply enlarge my awareness, seeking to notice God. We can do the same in our ministries, allowing the sound of the front door, the water faucet in the sink, or the voices of young people to remind us of God's presence. We can use images like smiles, eyes, bookbags, or baseball caps to remind us to notice God. I've even drawn a cross on my hand to remind myself to notice God during my activities with youth. Every time I noticed the cross, I allowed my heart to rest in the awareness that God was present.

Over time I've noticed that these interior glances keep me in my heart. They keep me attentive to God and remind me of my desire to be hospitable to young people. I find myself more and more aware of God's presence (or at least my desire for God's presence) within my daily life and interactions with young people. I've found that even when I forget to remember God, God prods my heart, reminding me to look and see that I'm not alone, that God's love is present and available.

# The Awareness Examen

Another historic Christian prayer that can help expand our presence with young people is the "awareness examen" or the "examination of conscience." The examen was part of a series of spiritual exercises that Ignatius of Loyola discovered through his own spiritual conversion. The spiritual exercises of Ignatius became the founding formational experience for the Jesuits and are used widely today by all walks of

Christians for spiritual growth and discernment.[16] Of all the practices and exercises he employed in the Jesuit community, Ignatius felt the examen was the most essential.

Over my eight years of consulting with churches across the country, I've found the examen to be a powerful practice for helping youth workers, parents, and congregations become more aware of the Holy Spirit and more present to young people. The examen invites us to spend time looking back over our encounters with young people, noting when we were most open and loving toward God and youth, and when we were "forgetful" or closed to God's love. Just as you might lie in bed at night considering the experiences of your day, this prayer asks you to review a particular encounter with young people and prayerfully ask two questions[17] :

*For what moment am I most grateful?*

*For what moment am I least grateful?*

These two questions, prayerfully invited, help us to identify moments of consolation and desolation. *Consolation* is a classical term used over the centuries by praying Christians to identify moments when we are more open to God, ourselves, and others. These are moments of connection, moments when we feel more alive, more transparent to God, and more loving toward other people. *Desolation* refers to the opposite experience—disconnection, depletion, alienation, a sense of being blocked to the presence of God, others, or ourselves. By paying attention to these two moments in our lives, we become more aware of the revelatory nature of our experience. Sometimes we notice patterns or occasions when we are in the flow of God's love; other times we see moments when we seem to be caught up in our own wounds and blindness.

After an activity or encounter with young people, I've found it helpful to look back and remember all the moments of gratitude, moments when I was open and receptive to God. Then I recall the

---

[16] *The Spiritual Exercises* were written for retreat leaders and spiritual directors who had experienced the 30 day retreat. It is not recommended reading without first experiencing the exercises with a knowledgeable retreat leader.

[17] *Sleeping with Bread*, Dennis Linn, Sheila Fabricant Linn and Matthew Linn (Paulist Press, 1995). These two questions come from the Linns' simple description of the awareness examen and its application to daily life. The Linns offer other questions such as, "When today did you receive and give the most love?"

moments of least gratitude, moments when I was blocked in some way to the presence of God and young people. Over time, as I've reflected on these consolations and desolations, I've found that I have become better attuned to the movement of the Holy Spirit in my ministry and better able to be my true self with kids.

Take a moment to set aside your reading and experience the prayer of examen. Find a place where you can pray without interruption. Light a candle to focus your attention and remind yourself of God's presence. Then spend a few moments in silence, allowing yourself to become aware of God's presence and care for you. When you're ready, ask the Holy Spirit to accompany you as you review your last encounter with young people. It might be a formal activity like Sunday school or youth group, or an informal interaction with youth in your family or community. As you recall your experience, let the following question arise: For what moment am I most grateful? Allow little things to emerge: a smile, a greeting, a kind word, sunlight in the room, an engaging conversation. Stay with whatever moment God seems to give you. Don't force anything—just be open and let the moment arise that seems to hold the most gratitude.

Let all else fall away as you spend a few moments holding this experience of gratitude. What did the experience feel like? What were you like? What were the youth like? What might God be seeking to teach you through this experience? You might want to journal some of these insights.

Now go back over your experience with youth and ask: For what moment am I least grateful? Again allow God to bring your attention to whatever moment seemed most filled with desolation. Take a few minutes to prayerfully journal what you've noticed.

In one church in which I volunteered with the youth ministry, a group of adults would engage in the awareness examen after each gathering with the high school youth group. Over time we noticed that greeting the kids as they arrived at the church was almost always cited as a "gratitude." For some reason, just saying "hello" and welcoming the kids into the building was a moment when we felt more transparent to God's presence and more real and authentic toward the youth. We began to discuss what this meant. We went through Scripture and noticed the hospitality of Jesus. Over time we sensed a call to extend this greeting time. There were eight adults in the ministry at that time, and we decided that each young person who entered the church would be greeted by each one of us. We would each take a moment to approach the young person, call her by name, chat a bit, and in some appropriate way make physical contact—a handshake, a pat on the back, a hug. Six months later the greeting time had extended to almost 20 minutes. To this day I'm convinced many of those kids came to that church just so they could walk through the door and experience eight adults calling out their name, touching their hand, and beaming at them with love. It was the awareness examen and our noticing of the power of the greeting time that pointed us in this direction.

I received an e-mail from Tim, a youth worker who began to practice the awareness examen after each youth group gathering. He relayed the following experience:

> During youth gatherings I would lead the kids in games, singing, and Bible study. As I spent time praying the examen, I noticed the moments of desolation always occurred during the singing. This surprised me, since I love to play guitar and Christian music was integral to my own faith formation. And yet, time after time group singing showed up as a moment of "least gratitude." When the time came for singing at the next youth

meeting, I decided to first stop and ask the young people if they enjoyed singing. It became quiet at first, then one young woman blurted out, "Well, it seems like this really isn't a time when we're all singing." She hesitated, then continued, "It seems like you're performing. Like you're having a great time singing these songs and we're supposed to listen to you...instead of sing along." I was shocked and embarrassed at first, but then realized the truth of what had been said. From that point on, I invited other kids to bring instruments and help plan the music and together lead singing. I'm grateful the examen helped me notice this place of disconnection. Now I feel I've been able to create something with the kids that feels much closer to what God wants for us.

While I was in seminary, I served as the volunteer youth director for a local Presbyterian church. Although the church and seminary were in an upper-middle class neighborhood, after a few years the youth ministry began to attract a number of underprivileged kids. These students were often rough in appearance and sometimes in behavior. Some of them were separated from their parents and living in foster homes. Others lived in government housing and had parents struggling to survive. A few of the kids had been in trouble with the law or suspended from school. After youth meetings the other leaders and I would discuss our anxiety regarding the influx of kids who often were disruptive and needy. Our conversations were frequently filled with concern about how to address the behavior of these "rough" kids.

remembering

Then we would pray the examen over our meeting. Time after time we'd discover that the presence of these "troubled" kids was our greatest consolation. Somehow their presence made the ministry more relevant, less frivolous. We noticed that many of the other kids from wealthier backgrounds were inundated with activities—for them youth group was just "one more thing." On the other hand, these new kids, even though they could be disruptive, were deeply invested in the group. They engaged wholeheartedly in discussions, prayed fervently, and soaked up attention from the ministry leadership. Instead of identifying these kids as troublemakers, we began to see them as a sign that Jesus was present in our group.

## Returning Home

Every time we remember God's presence, every time we remember to act from our true selves, every time we're reminded to open and receive a young person, we experience a little homecoming. Meister Eckhart once said, "God is at home, it's we who've gone out for a walk." These exercises remind us to look homeward, to turn and notice that the kingdom of God is among us (and within us).[18]

As we seek to live in the awareness of God, we often discover patterns of forgetfulness. We notice addictions to activity, reactions to particular kids who make us feel anxious or angry. When we allow God to expand our awareness, but we not only become aware of God's presence and our capacity to love, we also become more aware of our brokenness and propensity to shut God out. These sometimes painful revelations can also be useful. They can help us see ways in which we are still in need of healing. They can help point out our resistances to God or particular young people. It's helpful to notice the places within us that are needy, resistant, or unfinished. We can bring a gentle compassion to these aspects of ourselves, asking God to heal the broken

[18] Luke 17:21

contemplative youth ministry

or wounded places so we might become more authentic in our lives and our ministry with young people.

Seeking to expand our presence to God and young people can be a trying endeavor. We need to give ourselves permission to try a variety of exercises that help remind us of God's life among us. Sometimes we'll discover a particular exercise, sound, or image that helps us abide in Christ throughout our encounters with youth. Then we may find ourselves forgetting for weeks on end, caught up in our own activity and sense of importance. Or we may find ourselves stuck and notice that a particular exercise isn't bearing fruit. So we begin again. We try something else. We turn to God once more and pray, "Help me to remember you in this ministry." And then we trust. We forget again. We pray. We try again. And over time a shift occurs. We notice ourselves remembering more often than before that we're not alone, that the ministry is being carried, and that there is rest even in the most stressful of situations, because Jesus is both beside us and before us, making a way.

remembering

# forming the beloved
# community

# 9

A contemplative approach to youth ministry has been for me a rediscovery of community. I've learned to no longer do youth ministry alone. Before this I had always convinced myself it was easier to do things by myself—and to a certain extent, some of it is easier alone. However, the easier way or the quicker way is most definitely NOT the better way. In taking the very slow road of community and listening to one another's pain and joy...each person's story...we get to a safe place where each is valued and we can work together in mutual support seeking out the unique gifts each person brings to the table. Our youth have truly resonated to this reality.

—CHRIS BERTHELSEN, PASTOR, FIRST LUTHERAN CHURCH, ST. PAUL, MINNESOTA

One cannot be concerned about the spirituality of teens without being at the same time concerned about the spirituality of the entire community...the message embodied in a community's WAY is more powerful than any message in a textbook or on a blackboard. And is not this the problem that persons dealing with youth have been encountering again and again in recent years: finding a community that will embody the gospel in such a way that young people can recognize the presence of Jesus?

—MICHAEL WARREN, *YOUTH AND THE FUTURE OF THE CHURCH*

No matter how earnest our desire is to pray and be present to youth, our ministries will be short-lived if they aren't grounded in relationships with other Christians. It takes a greenhouse to nurture the souls of young people—a greenhouse formed by adults who want to know God. A young person's faith is best tended by a variety of relationships within a Christian community. Yet, sadly, youth ministry is one of the most isolated ministries in the church. If we seek to form a contemplative youth ministry, the participation of the wider church community is essential.

Dietrich Bonhoeffer once wrote that there is no such thing as an individual Christian. If we seek to share the life of Jesus with young people, we can't do it alone. Christians believe it's only as we gather together that we truly embody the Spirit of Jesus. Together we become his eyes, hands, mind, and heart.

A friend of mine from the Claremont School of Theology once interviewed a group of pastors from Southern California. These pastors were diverse in their denominational, racial, ethnic, and theological backgrounds. They led churches that varied in size, practice, and congregational make up. Yet when my friend asked these pastors what kind of youth minister they wanted for their churches, the answer was the same: a 20 something, attractive, guitar-playing, charismatic, youth-savvy, hip, hard-working, van-driving, free-spirited, denominationally-loyal, Jesus-loving, Bible-carrying, old-people-friendly, faith-filled, fiscally responsible, youth leader (preferably male with decorative facial hair and a mountain bike strapped to his car roof—or, if he's unavailable, a spunky, to-die-for, fashion-conscious female who will cry once on youth Sundays and twice on summer mission trips).

These Southern California pastors, like those in almost every church I know of, pray for the coming of the youth ministry messiah. They wait for that dynamo of a young adult who can relieve parents and church members of their burdensome youth, take away

forming the beloved community

141

all the anxiety over the junior high Sunday school class, and offer forgiveness to church members saying, "Come to me all you who are heavy burdened and I will give you rest. Your ridiculous attempts at ministry are washed away and forgotten. I release you from all guilt and responsibility. I, the savior to adolescents, am all that is needed. Go now in peace and worry not for your children, for they are safe in my tan and well-defined arms."

Like the Israelites who grew tired of attending to the mystery of God's presence in their midst, our churches shout and pray to the Lord, "Give us a king! A leader! Or at least someone who can decipher hip-hop lyrics!" Adults see the television images. We see the new fashions. We understand there are new forms of music and technologies. And we know we are hopelessly uncool. We still own eight-track tapes. Our clothing style is circa 1985. Our roller skates have two rows of wheels. And we fear there's no way youth will want to have anything to do with The Lord, Our God, if the Christians they know look more like disciples of The Wal-Mart, Our Discount Store. Yet didn't Jesus gather an ordinary, uneducated, uncool, working-class group of fishermen to help awaken the world to the love of God? There are youth ministers who are incredibly gifted in communicating the gospel to young people, but if these ministers don't have a group of Christians committed to serve beside them, they will soon burn out.

## Ministry of the Beloved Community

No matter how faithfully we pray and befriend young people—no matter how young, hip, capable, or "contemplative" we become—if we follow Jesus, we cannot minister to kids alone. I've watched numerous well-meaning parents, youth ministry volunteers, and paid professionals quickly burn out after seeking to share faith with youth by themselves. The energy of young people, the struggles of families, the odd hours, the isolation from the rest of the adults, the enormous task of passing on the intimacies of our faith to youth—all of these factors and more are too heavy for any one person to bear without shutting down or treating youth as projects.

In youth ministry circles, we often forget that ministry is to be done with others. We forget that Moses was given a community of elders to help lead the people of Israel. We forget that Jesus began his ministry by gathering Andrew and Simon Peter and the rest of the disciples. We overlook the fact that Paul and the other early missionaries almost always traveled in twos when they went to share the gospel. How can we teach young people that the Christian faith is about community when we're often alone in our ministry? How can we ask youth to break out of their cliques and befriend other students when they see us often isolated from other adults? How can we ask them to open up and share their life experiences with one another when they notice that we don't have a peer group of our own that shares our faith and life struggles?

A ministry done with others is a ministry of presence. Jesus tells us, "Where two or three are gathered in my name, I am there among them" (Matthew 18:20). Jesus reminds us that if we're to reveal the reality of God, we must be grounded in relationship. When we minister together, Jesus assures us that he is there—present and moving among us. If our ministries seek to communicate the nearness of God, we can't just rely on our own solitary contemplative practice; we must practice our prayer within a community that shares a calling to befriend youth.

A communal ministry not only bears the presence of Christ, it also allows for greater relationships with young people. I consider myself a very "youth-friendly" guy. I've spent lots of time with teenagers and have discovered I can relate to many different types of youth. However, no matter how well I listen, no matter how friendly or funny I am, there are many kids who just don't connect with me—as well as a significant number of kids who just plain don't like me. When we

forming the beloved community

minister with others, youth are presented with a diversity of relationships within the beloved community. A young person befriended by a
middle-aged receptionist, a 20-year-old college student, a retired bank
manager, and a young parent of a toddler—all who seek to live and
share the Christian life—will have a much richer image of Jesus, a
wider understanding of Christian community, and a more encouraging sense of her own place in God's family than if she were ministered
to by one person.

When we minister with youth together, we share the burdens
of ministry. There are more of us to take on the work of teaching,
befriending, organizing outings, and praying for kids. In my first four
years of youth ministry, at a fairly typical suburban church, I was overwhelmed by the issues young people brought to me: divorce, custody
battles, sexual abuse, self-mutilation, suicidal thoughts, issues of sexual identity, questions about vocation—and I haven't even mentioned
the spiritual questions I encountered! I wouldn't have been able to
respond to most of these issues if I hadn't gathered other adults to
minister alongside me.

When we minister together, we're also able to better discern and
follow the movement of the Holy Spirit. Discernment refers to the
process of sifting, weighing, and distinguishing what is of God and
what is not. Discernment is about locating and staying close to the
presence of Jesus. Discernment is about drawing close to God, locating ourselves in God, and then seeing how the Spirit is drawing us to
live and act. Discernment is critical to the Christian life and ministry.
Yet in order to discern, we need others. It is in community that we
hear God most clearly. Each of us has gaps in our spiritual hearing; we
need others to help us notice when we've gone deaf or are drowning
out God.

Finally, it's in community that we become our true selves. Youth
are hungry for authentic relationships with adults, yet it's incredibly
difficult for ministers and adults to be authentic among young people.

When we engage youth in ministry, we often want to be a role model; we want to project a faith life that has eliminated all doubts. We want to offer kids an endless well of time, energy, and compassion. These desires and projections not only come from us, but they also emanate from our churches and from young people themselves. It often seems everyone expects us to be super-human in our relationships with kids.

We need to minister in community so we can become real, so we can touch the ground and be reminded of our frailty. It is neither healthy nor biblical to minister without a group of people who can listen to our doubts, point out our shortcomings, and remind us of our belovedness in God. There are many times when it's appropriate to hold back some of our personal lives from the youth we serve; however, I've found that if I don't have a group of people who are committed to sharing my life, I become more and more distant in my relationships with teenagers and with God.

There are countless other reasons why Jesus asks us to minister in community—so we might help one another resist the violent hyperactivity of the culture, so we might carry one another's burdens, and so we might have greater wisdom in accompanying young people. But the primary question for many of us who work with youth isn't about the value of ministering with others; it's about how to find a community of people who are willing to take on this ministry. Today's youth are being abandoned by adults in a way no previous generation has ever experienced. Consider these words from sociologist Christian Smith in his thorough study on the spiritual and religious lives of teens:

> Significant numbers of teens today live their lives with little but the most distant adult direction and oversight. They spend the greater part of most weekdays in schools surrounded almost exclusively by their peers. Their parents are working

forming the beloved community

and otherwise busy. Members of their extended family live in distant cities. Their teachers are largely preoccupied with discipline, classroom instruction, and grading. Their neighbors tend to stay out of each others' business. These teens may have their own cars, cell phones, spending money, and televisions in their bedrooms. Or they may simply spend all their free time hanging out with friends and associates at the mall, on the streets, at friends' houses, or other places away from home. In any case, when school lets out, it may be hours before a parent gets home from work. If a teen works, his or her coworkers are mostly other teenagers who are also flipping burgers or working cash registers; their supervisors may be adults, but few teens have significant relationships with them beyond taking orders and collecting paychecks.[19]

There are few adults who have the time and willingness to be with young people, even their own teenagers. It's no different within the church. In my experience, most churches are desperate to find people willing to minister with youth. Most church members have been convinced that only the cool, the young, or the ignorant would dare enter a room full of 13-year-olds to teach them a faith that has been passed down for 2,000 years.

In contemplative youth ministry we're not just recruiting chaperones; we're seeking to form a group of people who will serve in the youth ministry as a "covenant community." We are looking for people who will see the ministry as part of their own spiritual growth. Just as a group of adults might gather within a church to pray or study the

contemplative youth ministry

[19] *Soul Searching: The Religious and Spiritual Lives of American Teenagers*, Christian Smith with Melinda Lundquist Denton (Oxford University Press, 2005), 185.

Bible, in contemplative youth ministry an adult community gathers to pray, share their lives, and serve the youth of their community.

# Gathering a Covenant Community

In my work to integrate prayer and relationship within youth ministry, I've developed a calling process for gathering adults to accompany young people on their journeys of faith. This process draws on a community's patience and trust in God. Over the past 10 years, I've seen this calling process help bring together youth ministry teams that pray, discern, deepen relationships, and serve together. These "covenant communities" tend the Spirit, keeping the sacred dimension of the Christian faith alive and available to young people. I've watched as youth ministries that previously involved one or two adults grow to include 18 to 20 adult volunteers as a result of this process. The volunteers in those ministries aren't treated as chaperones; they are treated as spiritual seekers—people who need prayer and friendship just as much as the young people do. Adults aren't simply asked to drive vans or read from a curriculum manual, they're asked to serve within a community of people who meet weekly for prayer, faith sharing, and discernment—as well as ministry with youth. (These meetings will be discussed further in chapter 10).

How do we gather adult volunteers? The following calling process was developed in order to gather a community of people who sense a call to share the way of Jesus with young people. This process is a discernment approach to volunteer recruitment. Although originally designed and tested for use in congregation-based youth ministries, this process may be useful within a variety of ministry settings. The heart of this process is listening. Pastoral leaders, congregations, and individual members are asked to listen prayerfully for whom the Spirit of God is calling within their community for accompany youth on the Way of Jesus.

Before you invite people to minister with kids, it's important to remember that you're seeking adults who have a sense of call to the ministry. You're not just looking for a warm body, you're seeking people who sense that their participation in ministry is intimately connected to God's movement in their lives. Make sure you recruit from diverse groups within your congregation. Consider inviting elderly people, parents, and even youth to serve. Be open to whomever God may choose.

Seek to embody a sense of trust as you engage in this process. Trust God and trust your congregation. Most recruiting in churches carries a sense of urgency and desperation. For example, read the following recruitment announcement that recently ran in the newsletter of a local church:

> WE NEED HELP! Fall is just around the corner and we still have nobody to teach our Middle School Sunday school class. IF WE DON'T HAVE A TEACHER BY AUGUST 20TH, WE WILL BE FORCED TO CANCEL THE CLASS. Call the church office if you or someone you know can do this important task!

It almost makes you want to run...far away. An announcement this desperate is frightening—and causes any and all who read it to assume the middle school students must be one terrible bunch of kids. What's sad is that someone will probably respond to the announcement out of guilt ("I didn't want the class to be cancelled!") and then carry resentment about getting stuck with serving.

A contemplative approach to recruiting relies on trust. We trust God will raise the people we need for the ministry. If that doesn't happen, then perhaps our church isn't called to youth ministry. Maybe our kids should attend the ministry next door or participate in the church in another way. We trust that the youth ministry is God's ministry; that God seeks to disciple young people; that God will lead, guide, and provide for this ministry.

We also trust our congregation. There's no need to rely on tricks, manipulation, or guilt to force people into serving youth. God will call the people to serve. And when they're called, we trust they will be the right people—even if they're not the people we'd choose. As I've practiced this calling process in a variety of churches, I'm amazed at the variety of adults who felt drawn to serve in the youth ministry. I've had churches that developed teams of eight to ten adults who were all over 50 years of age. I've seen some teams made up solely of parents and other ministry teams that had people ranging in ages from 14 to 83.

This process requires not only trust but also a commitment to listening. As we seek to gather together a ministry community, we listen with our hearts to the nudges and stirrings of the Spirit. Who is God calling to this ministry? How is the Spirit working among us? We listen to people without expectations, prejudgment, or anxiety. We seek to hear within each person we encounter the unique way in which God is moving and calling.

Finally, we must commit ourselves to prayer in this process. At regular intervals in our recruitment, we make space and time to direct our attention to God. Again and again we turn to God. What is it we want in this process? What is it God wants in this process? We take our attention off ourselves and our own expectations and we turn to God saying, "Your will be done."

# The Calling Process

The following steps outline a process for inviting the church community's involvement in youth ministry:

*Identifying Facilitators.* A minimum of two people should work together to call people to serve in the youth ministry. Preferably they should not be two staff members, but rather two people who seek to support and nurture the congregation's ministry with youth. Jesus always sent people out in pairs. It keeps the burden and focus off any particular individual.

*Prayer and Planning.* Once the two (or more) facilitators have been selected, they should begin their first meeting with prayer. This serves as a reminder that the focus of the process is not on them. Their role in this work is not to be successful, but simply to be faithful to what the Spirit is doing in their community. The prayer should go something like this:

> God, this is your church and your ministry, and these are your young people. Help us listen for the ways you are at work in our community. Help us not to be manipulative or anxious but to trust you as we seek to gather a community of people to serve in this ministry. Help us to be faithful to how you are calling us to serve in this process. Finally, we ask you to guide us in discovering the people you choose to raise up for this ministry. We pray all these things in Jesus' name. Amen.

*Listening to the Community.* The first task of the facilitators is to talk with as many people as possible in the congregation. These conversations can take place in informal settings such as coffee hour or more formal settings such as board meetings. The goal of this stage is for the facilitators to ask as many people as possible in the congregation the following question: *Who in this congregation enjoys young people and would make a good volunteer in the youth ministry?* It's important to invite people to think beyond age and social categories. Just because a person is retired, in high school, a parent, or has irregular church attendance doesn't mean she isn't called to youth ministry.

Often people will say things like, "Margie always tithes to the youth program, but she's 80 years old, and I don't know if she has the energy to work with the youth." Or "Chloe is good with kids, but she has two teens of her own, and I don't think it would be good for her to be involved in the ministry if her kids are in it." Or "Tom would be ideal, but I don't know about his commitment to ministry. He only shows up at church two or three times a year and mostly spends his time coaching the swim team." The rule at this stage of the process is to write down every name that is offered—no matter what qualifiers or misgivings are attached to that name. We don't know whom God is calling into this ministry, so we have to be open to all possibilities.

As the facilitators circulate this question throughout the congregation, they will begin to collect a list of names. Continue collecting names until you've spoken to most of the congregation. Avoid blanket recruitment announcements in newsletters or bulletins. It's important to make this process personal. Spend the time talking to people. God is in relationships, so make contact with people and let them in on the discerning process. Remember that it's an honor to serve in youth ministry—people who serve in youth ministry have the sacred task of passing on the intimacies of our faith to the next generation. You don't want just anybody to serve; you want people who are called.

*Meeting with the Pastor.* After the facilitators have gathered names, they should meet with the senior pastor. The pastor should look over the names of people listed and advise the facilitators of any names that should be removed from the list. (Pastors are often privy

forming the beloved community

151

to information about church members that might be important when calling people to work with youth.)

*Praying over the Names.* It's important to spend some time praying over the list of names. Keep God at the center of the selection process by regularly praying for the people drawn to the youth ministry. Facilitators might pray something like this:

> Holy God, help us to be faithful to you. Help us listen for the people you are calling into this ministry. This is your church, this is your ministry, and these are your young people. Help us listen and be faithful to the tasks you have given us. We pray for each of the people who have been named. We ask that you speak clearly to those you have called into this ministry. Help them discern the ways in which you are asking them to serve. Help us not to be manipulative but to be open and grateful as we speak with them. We trust you, and thank you for trusting us with your work. We pray all these things in Jesus' name. Amen.

*Setting Appointments with Potential Volunteers.* The facilitators then contact the people named by the community as potential volunteers for the ministry, beginning with those who were named more than once by the congregation. Make personal appointments with each of the people on the list. This takes time because often you must coordinate three or more schedules. The invitation to serve should not be left on an answering machine or given in a hallway conversation. We are asking people to discern a call to ministry; that call needs to be honored with time and space.

*Meeting with Potential Volunteers.* Two facilitators should meet together with each potential volunteer, preferably in a home or another environment that allows for personal conversation. The facilitators should get together a few minutes before meeting with a potential volunteer to pray and prepare themselves for the meeting.

*Presenting the Invitation.* Facilitators should explain to each potential volunteer that he or she has been named by the congregation as someone who has gifts in ministering with young people. Potential volunteers should understand that they are being asked to discern (to listen for) God's call to youth ministry. Facilitators should emphasize that the volunteers are not being asked to be chaperones or "answer people" but are being asked to engage in the youth ministry as a setting for their own spiritual growth. Facilitators should mention that each volunteer would be expected to be part of a community of volunteers who will meet regularly to pray, share, and discern. The time expectations should also be communicated clearly—often it's good to ask volunteers to serve for at least one year.

Meetings with potential volunteers should be relaxed and informal. Take the pressure off the meeting by encouraging people to say "no" if they feel uncomfortable or unable to accept the invitation for any reason. Trust that God will provide people for the ministry. Avoid using guilt or manipulation ("The kids totally love you; it will be such a disappointment if you don't participate").

Facilitators should not ask candidates for an answer at the initial meeting. Potential volunteers should be encouraged to pray about their call and discuss it with their family (especially if they are a parent of a teenager). Give people at least a week to pray and think it over before you contact them to hear their response. Spend time praying for folks as you give them time to discern. After a week or so, contact people either in person or by phone and listen to their response. Trust that each person is responding to his or her sense of God's call.

*Modifying the Call.* Often people will respond with a variety of modifications to the original invitation to serve in the ministry: "I can't help out every week, but I could volunteer every other week." "Would it be okay to volunteer just for larger events like mission trips?" "I'd be glad to help fix meals or drive, but I can't make a regular commitment to be part of the ministry team."

All such responses should be considered. Usually it's best to accept whatever time and energies people offer—as long as the facilitators make sure there is a critical mass of four to eight people who have said "yes" to serving as part of a regular ministry community.

*Identifying Advocates.* Often you'll find people who are supportive of youth ministry but don't feel called to work directly with young people. Perhaps they are elderly, have a child in the youth group, or have some other reason that prevents their hands-on involvement. I've found these people can be very valuable to the ministry as "advocates."

Advocates are part of the ministry community, although they don't actually work with youth. They attend youth leader meetings. They pray, discern, and even help plan the youth ministry, but aren't expected to engage in the youth activities. Advocates can help remind the ministry team of the larger church context, looking for ways in which the ministry can integrate its work with the life of the church as a whole. At the same time, when advocates are among the larger congregation, they seek to remind the congregation of the activities, interests, and struggles of the youth ministry. In this way advocates are bridge builders—fostering connections between the youth ministry and the wider congregation.

Advocates can play a valuable support role within the ministry without being enmeshed in all its relationships and tasks. It's good to have at least one advocate on your team to help give the ministry an outside perspective.

*Celebration.* After the team has been called, plan a gathering with everyone—volunteers, ministers, youth, and facilitators—to celebrate the end of the calling process and the faithfulness of the volunteers' responses to the call.

Because this process asks congregations to take time for prayer, discernment, and personal relationship, it is a much slower form of recruitment. Churches I've observed have spent anywhere from one to six months in this process. It takes time to meet, talk, pray, listen, discern, and then make decisions as to who is called into the youth ministry.

Feel free to modify the process based on the unique character of your congregation. You may want to host a meal for all potential volunteers and present the ministry invitation to them all at once. Some churches have held a special dinner in a home and distributed hand-made invitations and other personal touches that communicated the respect and gratitude the church had for the potential volunteers.

Once your community of adults has been gathered, it's good to hold a retreat where people can pray together, get to know one another, and talk about the way in which they hope to serve young people. I've put suggestions for a sample volunteer retreat in the appendix of this book.

Every church I've worked with that has used this recruitment process has increased the number of adults in their youth ministry. Depending on the size of the church, most congregations have gathered anywhere from 8 to 22 volunteers. The first church I worked with while using this process ended up calling 20 adults to serve weekly in the youth ministry—out of a congregation of only 150 members. Five years later 15 of those adults were still serving. Imagine the experience of young people when they engage in a youth ministry in which 8 to 20 adults pray for them, seek to be present to them, and respond to their spiritual needs and questions. This is the kind of ministry Jesus established, a group of people called together to pray and serve, to share the good news of God's presence among us.

# the liturgy for discernment

**10**

When I think of the people who minister on our team—Lisa, Jennifer, Graham, and Paul—I feel more like they're my brothers and sisters than even my own blood. I have shared things with them that I haven't even told my wife. They bear my burdens and the burdens of ministry with me. The kids see our relationships, and I think it tells them more about the Christian life than what we're teaching them during lesson times.

—DOUG LADSEN, UTILITY LINEMAN, VOLUNTEER YOUTH WORKER, SARON UNITED CHURCH OF CHRIST, LINTON, INDIANA

Individual perception, reasoning, and understanding are always limited. Even a person who feels absolutely certain that a specific revelation comes from God may be mistaken as to how it is to be applied. Because God often reveals part of the picture to one person and another part to another person, it is prudent to consult one another to discern God's counsel, guidance, and direction, even if there is no apparent reason to do so. While circumstances sometimes require us to act without consulting others, the danger of arrogance and error in proceeding on our own can be great.

—SUZANNE FARNHAM, JOSEPH GILL, R. TAYLOR MCLEAN, & SUSAN WARD, *LISTENING HEARTS*

At 11:27 a.m. in the Myra T. Shipley Fellowship Room of First Friendly Church, youth minister Paul Lopez has the fixed smile of a professional customer service representative. It's the kind of smile that says, "I'm politely pretending to be listening to you, while I'm really thinking of something else." His eyes, glazed and unfocused, are pointed in the direction of Carl, a parent and youth ministry volunteer who for the third time this year is describing his college mentor...

"Now most of us assume an archeologist would be an ace in geography. But I'm telling you, during our trip to Israel, Dr. Carlton couldn't tell the hills of Jericho from a hill of beans!" [Dramatic pause] "Did I ever tell you about what happened when we tried to find the Sea of Galilee?"

"Yes," Paul says weakly, knowing it will have no effect.

"Well, Dr. Carlton was supposed to meet me at the northeast shore of the Galilean Sea..."

Paul is not listening. Paul is thinking of the work he has to do to prepare for the weekend youth retreat. He steals a glance at his watch, realizing he will be stuck in this meeting for at least another two hours. Paul is silently praying, pleading with God, "Please, Lord, make him stop. Don't let him tell the whole story. Lord, I'm only paid for 20 hours a week to do this job. Please don't let two of them be wasted on this meeting."

Margaret, the middle school Sunday school teacher, breaks in, "Speaking of doctors, I know I said this last week, but let me say it again, there is no way I can continue to lift those chairs to set up that classroom. My back can't take it anymore. I was on an 800-milligram prescription of ibuprofen, but now the doctor thinks I need to switch to extra strength aspirin. Well, my sister tried that and..."

A small tear rolls slowly down Paul's face. "How long must I suffer, how long will you test my patience, O Lord?"

Across the street at Second Church of the Lord, Polly Gilbert quickly takes her seat in the youth room. She looks at the clock on the wall: 7:01. Following a brief prayer, the director of Christian education opens the meeting, "Good morning, everyone. Before we begin I want to remind each of you to keep your report to five minutes or less. Last week we went 15 minutes over schedule. Only share those items that are relevant to the whole group." He gives Polly a quick glance.

Polly looks at her notes and scratches out "mom's illness" and "prayers for Allison." She sits with her head down trying to hold back her tears. *I feel so out of place. I don't know what I'm doing with the youth. My mother is back in the hospital. I still can't believe that Allison, one of our most active high school girls, has been cutting her arms. I'm overwhelmed...*

"Polly? Polly? What do we need to know from our youth ministry department?"

There are two primary methods for running a staff meeting in North American congregations. The first is what I call the "chaos" approach. A chaos meeting is open and informal. It moves and shifts based on the whims and moods of the group. The length and content of the meeting vary wildly. One week the staff is engaged in a heated two-hour discussion on cleaning supplies. The next week a volunteer parent spends 45 minutes sharing about her mother's trip to Canada. There is a "feeling" of attending to relationships, yet few people are really listening. Most are simply talking, dumping out whatever thoughts, tensions, or issues they happen to be carrying that day.

In contrast to the chaos meeting is the "control" approach. Based on business models, this staff meeting is focused on efficiency and production. The meeting is more formal and structured, with everyone attending to the clock. Staff members come ready to do business, setting their personal lives aside. Control meetings focus on concrete items—numbers, budgets, goals, and tasks. The focus of control meetings is to get more work done faster. Personal sharing, brainstorming, and open discussion are left for subgroups.

Most congregations—and most youth ministry leaders—tend toward either a chaos approach or a control approach to staff meetings. Yet neither of these extremes—nor the continuum that lies between them—is grounded in Christian living. New youth ministry volunteers who step into either of these meetings will quickly become disillusioned and demoralized. The center of Christian communities should be neither corporate efficiency nor personal free-for-alls. Instead, there should exist a spiritual community—a covenant group that is attentive to God, discerning of the Spirit, and caring for one another. In youth ministry our methods are as significant as our message. If our meetings are focused on personalities or productivity, we'll tend to measure the success of the ministry based on how many youth attended each event and whether kids like the youth leaders.

In 1997 I designed a different approach to staff meetings, a process that seeks to place prayer, relationships, and discernment as the primary tasks of a Christian meeting. This process has been used throughout the partner congregations in the Youth Ministry and Spirituality Project. It is a process based on prayer, relationships, and deep listening.

The "liturgy for discernment" is a form of communal discernment. The word *liturgy* comes from the Greek word *leitourgia*, which means "the work of the people." In the Christian tradition this word has usually referred to worship, but it can also be understood more broadly as the way we gather in the presence of God.

Discernment is the process of listening for the voice of God. For Christians, discernment refers to "testing the spirits"—the process of seeking and discovering what is of God and what is not (1 John 4:1ff). Discernment is an art, a skill, and a gift. It requires a desire not only to know God's call, but to follow God's leading. Discernment requires humility, a willingness to set aside our own plans, agendas, and aspirations (this is often referred to in the tradition as "holy indifference") so we might be free to respond to God's bidding. We need humility in discernment, not only in relation to God, but also so we might be open to the input of others. As Christians we trust that God is most clearly heard through and in the midst of other followers of Jesus. Discernment is also mindful of Jesus. We discern in relationship to Scripture, watching how our sense of God's calling resonates with the life of Jesus.

Discernment is not a one-time event, but an ongoing practice. We return again and again, constantly seeking to deepen our awareness of God's presence and calling. The hope of discernment is that over time our lives and ministries will become more transparent to God's life and more faithful to Jesus' way of love. No matter how sincere we are in our discernment, the truth is we can never be certain we're encountering God's presence or following God's call. We'll never, in this life, definitively know God's call; that's why we call it Christian "faith." Yet often when we look back, we notice signs of God's presence and our own faithfulness.

The "liturgy for discernment" is a communal practice that invites us into deeper cooperation with the Spirit in the midst of the work of ministry. The liturgy was originally designed for people engaged in youth ministry, but it can also be used whenever Christians gather to do the work of God. The liturgy changes the tone and spirit in which the "business" of ministry is done. The liturgy invites an atmosphere of prayer and listening, rather than one focused only on efficiency and productivity. In contrast to other approaches to ministry, this process emphasizes deepening relationships—with oneself, with others, and with the Spirit of God. My experience has been that when people spend time in prayer and relationship building, the ministry becomes a great source of nourishment; people enjoy the ministry, serve with greater authenticity, and stay involved longer. One church I've worked with in Oregon called 18 adults to the youth ministry. After meeting each week for seven years and engaging in the liturgy of discernment, these same 18 adults are still serving in the youth ministry. Imagine the continuity and stability the youth feel in that ministry.

The liturgy for discernment has two basic movements. In the first half of the meeting, the process moves inward, centering the group in relationships. Through ritual, conversation, listening, and prayer, the group is reconnected with their own hearts, one another, and the Spirit of God among them. These relationships are then focused on the call, or central identity, of the group. This is the pivotal point of the meeting, when the group's attention moves outward, reflecting on its collective sense of identity and God's call ("Who are we and how is God calling us?"). Business items are then responded to within this deeper awareness of self, others, God, and call (or group purpose). As the group practices this way of doing ministry, its members begin to operate less and less as a business committee, and more and more as a spiritual community. Lives are shared, relationships are built, spirits are formed, and gifts are exercised.

Go back to the two ministry team meetings described at the beginning of the chapter. See if you can get a sense of how these meetings might be different if they were focused on prayer, deep listening, and discernment:

At 11:27 a.m. in the Myra T. Shipley Fellowship Room of First Friendly Church, youth minister Paul Lopez enters the room. The other six members of his youth ministry team have already arrived and are seated in a circle chatting amicably. Paul smiles and greets people, then lights a candle in the middle of the group and says out loud, "We light this candle as a reminder of Christ's light and presence here among us." A gentle silence falls over the group. Paul takes

the liturgy for discernment

his seat, closes his eyes, and catches his breath after a busy morning. He takes a moment to remember that God is present beneath the stress of the upcoming youth retreat. After a few minutes of silence, Carl, a parent and volunteer, says, "Lord, we've got a lot going on this week. We ask that you help us listen to what you want us to do. Help us in our planning with these kids. They need you, Lord. And we do too. Amen."

Paul addresses the group: "Let's take a moment, as we do each week, just to check in. Let's each take a minute or two to tell one another how we're doing. As each of us shares, we'll ask that the rest of the group remain in silence. We want to keep from falling into conversation. Just listen with care to how each person is doing today."

There is silence for a minute or two. Then Carl shares that he just got his pictures back from Israel, and he's still overwhelmed by the whole experience. It wasn't what he expected, yet the crowds and craziness of the whole trip has made him see the Bible in a new way.

Carl finishes and the group returns to silence. Then Margaret starts to speak. She's worried about her back. The last visit to the doctor was unsettling. It seems like no one knows what the problem is. She's worried she might have to have surgery. She feels a little depressed that she can't do the things she used to be able to do.

Margaret finishes and the group returns to silence. Then Paul shares that he feels very stressed about the upcoming retreat. One of the parent drivers cancelled last night and there aren't enough cars to get everyone to the camp. The food still hasn't been purchased, and he feels frustrated that he hasn't had time to prepare the teaching sessions for the retreat. "I have a lot of anxiety at this meeting," he shares, "because I'm worried we're not going to get the preparations done in time."

Judy, a college student, shares that her week has been pretty good. She went to the lake with some friends and had a great time. It was nice to get away from school. She's looking forward to the retreat as another chance to escape school and an opportunity to deepen her relationship with some of the sophomore girls.

When all of the sharing has ended, Paul asks Carl to lead the group in *lectio divina*. Carl reads Mark 4:35-41, an account of Jesus and the disciples in a storm. He reads the passage three times. The group falls into silent prayer for 10 minutes. Then Carl asks people to share from the prayer.

Again there is silence. Then Judy begins to speak: "'Asleep on the cushion' is what stood out to me. How could Jesus be asleep on the cushion? I almost started to laugh. I mean the world is in trouble, there's a storm, everybody's freaked out, and he's sleeping. I just think there's something cool about that. It's like deep down everything is going to be okay."

There's quiet, and then Paul speaks: "The word 'awe' is what came to me. 'Awe.' I really want to have a sense of 'awe' in my life. I feel like I spend so much time doing all these little details that I never stand back and just take it all in. I could just feel that this weekend I need to take a walk outside or something and just remember to be in 'awe' at Jesus."

Others share their words and insight. After everyone has spoken, Paul says, "Okay, well, given all that we've shared, how do we sense God calling us?" No one speaks for a minute or two. Then Margaret says, "I'm still thinking about Judy saying she felt like laughing. I mean, the other disciples would've been really angry if you were on that boat and started laughing during the storm. But I think Jesus would've been right there with you, laughing alongside you. I think about our kids. Every time I go into that youth room they're horsing around and laughing. They love to laugh. I think that's why I serve in this ministry. Somehow they cheer me up and remind me of the lighter side of life." She pauses for a moment. "So I just think we all

the liturgy for discernment

need to lighten up more. I think we need to go on the trip this weekend and have fun with these kids. We need to laugh with them and let them know we trust that God is here and everything is going to be all right—even if we don't find another van driver or, I guess, even if the doctors can't get my medication right."

The group talks about Margaret's insight for a few minutes, and then Paul says, "Well, let's keep these insights and our prayer in the room as we look at the work we have to do for this retreat." The group then begins to look over the tasks for the upcoming retreat and make plans. After 30 minutes or so, Paul asks Margaret to close the meeting in prayer. The group stands, holds hands, and Margaret prays: "Resting Jesus, help us hear your laughter this weekend. Help us carry you, resting in our hearts as we go about the work of this ministry. And most importantly, help us share a sense of awe and wonder with the young people—awe and wonder at who you are. Thank you, Jesus. Amen."

Notice the different pace of the meeting and the space given for silence, sharing, and prayer. The work of the ministry was addressed, but only after the group had centered itself in prayer and relationship. This is only an example, so it appears less messy than if you were to watch a real ministry team engaged in this process. But the connections between the prayer and the group's call, as well as the sense of moving from anxiety to a sense of peace about the work, are common among the groups I've observed in this process.

And what might happen at the "all business, all the time" church in our second example? What if Polly could carry her concerns about her mother and the kids of her youth group into a church meeting that honored prayer and relationship? How would Polly's sense of isolation and doubt shift if she were allowed to bring her whole self to the table? How would she feel about her vocation as a youth minister if she had the support of others who shared her struggles in the ministry, her suffering over her mother, and her prayer for the wounded kids in the youth group?

# A Circle of Trust

The liturgy for discernment offers a process for group gatherings that emphasizes a "circle of trust."[20] Such a process involves careful listening to ourselves, to one another, and to the call of the Spirit. Below is a step-by-step description of the movements in the liturgy for discernment.

**Ritual.** As people gather to meet, there is an opening ritual. This should be a simple activity that draws the group's attention to the presence of God. It could be a song, a moment of silence, or the lighting of a candle. The ritual consecrates the meeting, changing the context from ordinary time and space to sacred time and space. The ritual announces to the group, "We are coming into an awareness of the Presence of God." Avoid pastoral prayers or other rituals that rely on the gifts of only one person. The ritual should be repeatable no matter who is in attendance. The ritual should last no longer than a couple minutes.

**Relating.** This is a time for building relationships within the community. Each member of the group is asked, "How are you?" and is given one to two minutes to check in. (That may not seem like much time, but when real listening is present, people tend to be more mindful of their words, making it possible to share a lot in a brief amount of time.) This is a time of deep listening, of attending to one another. Jesus says there are only two things required of Christians, to love God and to love one another as we love ourselves (Mark 12:28-34). In this time we love others through our eyes and ears. We listen without interrupting or commenting. We leave silence after each speaker to honor what has been said. The hope is that in the midst of silence and careful listening the speaker is able to hear herself, and thus is able to speak from a deeper place. At times you may want to change

[20] I borrow this phrase from Parker Palmer's *A Hidden Wholeness: The Journey Toward an Undivided Life.* Palmer defines a "circle of trust" as a group whose intent is to make it safe for the soul to show up and offer us guidance.

the liturgy for discernment

the check-in question to something like, "How is your faith being nurtured in this ministry?" or "How is your family life?"

This time is valuable because it allows people to drop whatever baggage they may be carrying (joys or anxieties). The sharing helps create more space within them to pray and focus on the work of the group. Youth ministry teams who hold these meetings right before they gather with young people have found that this sharing allows them to clear out (or touch into) anger, frustration, or other distractions that might otherwise come out unconsciously among the youth.

**Receiving.** After listening to one another, we turn our attention more fully to God. This is a time of prayerful listening—full attentiveness to the Spirit of God within and among us. The prayer makes room for these three movements:

1. Centering: Our attention shifts from the particulars of the agenda to the One who calls us to this work. We remember who we are and Whose we are.
2. Transformation: In the silence we become available to God. A new word is given, wounds are tended, and renewal takes place.
3. Call: We get in touch with the Spirit's longing within us, our calling, and the unique way in which God has invited us to live and serve.

Either of the two forms of prayer described in the previous chapter can be used in this time of receiving. I have found it most effective to alternate the group's use of *lectio divina* and the awareness examen.

When the group uses *lectio divina*, a short passage of Scripture is selected for the prayer time. The passage can be chosen from the lectionary, the curriculum being used with the youth group, or selected specifically for the meeting. One person should explain the process of *lectio divina* to the group—being sure to tell the group how long the

contemplative youth ministry

silence will last. After a brief time of silent prayer, the leader slowly reads the passage aloud two times, urging each individual to listen for a word or phrase that jumps out. The group then observes 5 to 10 minutes of silence before the leader invites the team members to draw their attention back to the group. (For more on *lectio divina*, see chapter 5 or Thelma Hall's *Too Deep for Words* [Paulist Press, 1988].)

On alternate meetings the group replaces the *lectio* prayer with the awareness examen. Again the leader should begin by explaining the prayer to the group members and informing them how long the silences will last. The group is then invited to a time of silence. The leader then says, "Ask God to go with you over our last gathering with young people [or whatever other activity is the primary focus of the group] and consider the following question: *For what moment am I most grateful?*" After another few minutes of silence and contemplation, the leader then says, "As you're ready, ask God to go back with you over our last gathering with youth and consider, *For what moment am I least grateful?*" Allow a few more minutes of silence before inviting those gathered to draw their attention back to the group. (For more on the awareness examen, see chapter 8 or *Sleeping with Bread* by Dennis Linn, Sheila Fabricant Linn, and Matthew Linn [Paulist Press, 1995].)

**Ruminating.** In this movement the group takes time to listen to what each person noticed during the prayer time. If the group has prayed *lectio divina*, the leader might say something like, "I'd like to invite you to share the word that came to you in the prayer as well as any other insights." If the group does the awareness examen, the leader might say something like, "I'd like to invite each of us to share what came to us in the prayer, one moment where we were most grateful and one moment where we were least grateful." Allow each person to speak without interruption. This should be a time of deep listening to how God is speaking to the group.

the liturgy for discernment

**Reflecting.** We then take time to reflect on our call. In this movement we are moving out from our individual sharing to focus on our group identity and group purpose. Someone asks the following question to the group: "Given all that we've heard and shared, what is God's call to us?" (Some groups replace "call" with "invitation.") The group has an open conversation, allowing silence after each speaker. This is a moment for the group to remember its call and reflect on new words or insights that have come out of the prayer. This should take anywhere from 5 to 10 minutes.

**Responding.** The group then begins to address the business items on the agenda. But as the meeting moves ahead, it is important that the leader remind the group to continue to be aware of the prayer and sharing that has occurred.

**Returning.** At the end of the meeting, the group shares a closing prayer, returning its attention to the Spirit of God. Prayers of gratitude, intercession, and blessing may be offered.

It's important to realize from the start that this meeting format may not be as productive as other models for doing business (especially in an immediate sense). Secular business models discard relationships for efficiency; this model does just the opposite. At times people may get frustrated at the amount of time "wasted" on prayer, checking in, and silence. It may seem as though nothing is getting done. But the liturgy trusts that waiting on God isn't "doing nothing." Something is happening—it's just not under our control. The success of this approach is not measured by productivity; it's measured by fruits of the Holy Spirit, such as kindness, generosity, joy, and patience (Galatians 5:22-26). This doesn't mean we don't seek to be productive and mindful of people's time; it just means our first priority is prayer and relationship.

One way to make these meetings even more effective is to share the leadership among the youth ministry volunteers. Take turns leading the prayer or check-in. Find ways to make sure everyone participates in guiding the meeting. The meeting takes on a more communal atmosphere when different people are assigned the different parts of the liturgy. Some groups create a roster so people know weeks ahead of time when they will be responsible for the "Relating" question or the "Receiving" prayer.

Many youth ministry groups have found that meeting right before or right after a youth event is most effective. It helps group members prepare themselves to minister with the youth and stay close to the Spirit's leading.[21]

# Testimonies

For eight years I've watched youth ministries and congregations involved in the Youth Ministry and Spirituality Project be transformed as they engage in the liturgy for discernment. I've seen ministries that felt dead and isolated in a congregation come to life—not only with the Spirit of God, but with deepened relationships between adults and youth. As churches begin to create ministries grounded in prayer and relationship, it's not unusual for them to undergo fundamental transformations like the one described here by Chris Berthelson, a Lutheran pastor and parent of two from St. Paul, Minnesota:

> Before we began to practice the liturgy for dis-
> cernment, we had a youth room with a pool
> table right in the middle of it. The room looked
> like a recreation room. As we began to pray and
> share together and discuss the question, "What
> is God's call for us?" we began to sense that we
> needed to create a youth space that was more

[21] Two helpful resources in regards to communal discernment in ministry are *Listening Hearts: Discerning Call in Community*, by Suzanne G. Farnham, Joesph P. Gill, R. Taylor McLean and Susan M. Ward (Morehouse Publishing, 1991), and *Grounded in God: Listening Hearts Discernment for Group Deliberations*, by Suzanne G. Farnham, Stephanie A. Hall and R. Taylor McLean (Morehouse Publishing, 1996). Both of these books have excellent guidelines for ministry groups.

sacred and less focused on entertainment or recreation. We shared this with the kids and asked them to pray about it. We were totally surprised when they said they sensed the same thing. So together we dismantled the pool table and had a month of meetings in which we talked about sacred space. We did Bible studies on Moses and the Holy Land and other kinds of lessons that referred to sacred space. Eventually, one of the kids designed a big butterfly that we all painted on one of the walls. We repainted the room as part of a prayer service. When we finished, we all just sat in the room—adults and youth—in awe at what God had led us to do. Now when kids bring their friends to the youth room, they point out the verses and images on the walls. They tell them how the room used to be just a recreation room. They tell the other kids like they're telling them something sacred has happened. And something sacred has happened.

Another one of my favorite stories about the power of gathering people together to pray and discern on behalf of young people occurred in a small Episcopal church in a central Colorado ski town. The congregation was aging and at first resisted their new priest's attempts to create a youth ministry. As one elder told me, "We are a dying congregation. We need a hospice ministry not a youth ministry." The young priest asked the church vestry if he could spend a portion of his hours seeking to discover whether God was calling the congregation to form a ministry with youth. He agreed to abandon his efforts if the church were unable to establish a youth ministry within two years. The vestry reluctantly agreed, but warned him that he would be unable to find adults in the congregation to support such a ministry, much less to serve in it.

Father James and his wife, Eli, came to a training program in which I taught the calling process and liturgy for discernment. They went back to their parish and began to pray, discern, and share the vision of a youth ministry with other church members. Within a month they were pleasantly surprised to find eight adults—most of them elderly—in their 200-member congregation who sensed a call to youth ministry. After a day-long retreat, the group began to meet weekly, faithfully following the liturgy for discernment. Together they would pray, share their lives, and discern what actions they could undertake in order to welcome the town's young people into the church.

One year later I contacted James to ask how it was going. "Well, we haven't attracted any youth to the church yet," he responded. But he told me that after a year of prayer and sharing, the ministry team had noticed "home" was becoming a recurring theme and image. He told me they had really begun to care for one another and often met for dinner outside of their meetings. He told me two of the members had undergone severe family crises and that the group had worked hard to care for one another. However, he ended the conversation by telling me he was disappointed they still did not have a youth ministry. He was beginning to sense that he should direct his energy in other directions.

Two months later I was in Colorado and showed up at James's church a few minutes before worship. James spotted me and rushed over. "You're not going to believe what happened last night," he told me, bursting with excitement. "You'll have to hear it in worship." I went inside the sanctuary and sat down. After the prelude, James came to the front and told the congregation "something tremendous" had occurred that he needed to share.

One month earlier a young man had died of alcohol poisoning after a night of partying and drinking with his buddies. James had read about the tragedy in the paper. A few days later he was in a coffee shop when two guys in their early 20s noticed James wearing his white collar, came up to him, and asked if he were a priest. They then asked, "Do you do memorial services?" He told them he did, and invited them to sit down. James listened as they told him it was their friend who had died. Then they began to talk about their lives in Colorado. They told James that they and many of their friends came from broken homes, and many of them went from ski town to ski town looking for work and parties. They talked about sleeping in cars and working odd jobs in this upscale resort town. James continued to listen. They told him their friend was from New York, and that his parents had flown his body back home for the funeral. None of them had the money to go back East for the service. They asked James if he could hold some sort of memorial service in town so they could mourn the death of their friend. James agreed to do it and a date was set.

The next week James met with the youth ministry team. While they were sharing, he told them about the upcoming memorial service. He asked for volunteers to help prepare and serve food for the young people. Everyone agreed to help out. James said he expected a small gathering of 5 to 10 people. On the day of the service, the youth ministry team showed up early. They transformed the fellowship room of the church. They wanted it to feel like you were visiting your favorite grandmother's house. They placed homemade tablecloths, little bouquets of flowers, and bowls of candy on each of the tables. They had three kinds of soup simmering in the kitchen and fresh-baked cookies placed on platters around the room. They made sandwiches, cut them in triangles, and placed them on each table, ready for the group's arrival.

When it came time for the service, James said, "It was like the underbelly of our town showed up." Over 100 young adults, ages 16 to 25, gathered in the sanctuary wearing baggy pants, knit hats, worn military fatigues, and other rough snow gear. James ran back to the fellowship hall and told the youth ministry team to prepare more food. The group hurried to the grocery store and soon formed a sandwich assembly line while 68-year-old Glenda made another pot of corn chowder.

At the close of the service, James invited the youth to stay for food. Every one of them stayed. For the next five hours the young "ski bums" ate soup and sandwiches and poured their hearts out to the listening adults. One woman later told me, "Most of us have lived long enough to have friends and even close family die, so we knew how to listen and be with these kids who were in grief."

The adults noticed that many of the young people had holes in their shoes and clothes. They went over to the long-neglected "donation" box placed in the narthex of the church. They found clean pants, tennis shoes, and warm jackets. They brought them to the fellowship hall and offered them to the youth. They were ecstatic! When the evening finally started to wind down, one of the young men asked if they could come to the church again sometime.

That night, after clean-up, the youth ministry team gathered. They talked about the great need for food, friendship, and clothing among these discarded youth in their town. They talked about how much they had enjoyed talking and being with these young adults who often appeared rough and distant. They prayed. They listened to how God was calling them to serve. An idea emerged. Each month they would have a night like this—a night where they served good food, handed out clothing, and spent time just hanging out with these young adults.

As James stood in the front of the church that Sunday and told this story, he became emotional and said, "We have a ministry, people. We have a ministry. We need every one of you to buy groceries and bring them to the church. We need each of you to go through your closets and bring any shoes, pants, and warm clothes you can spare. We need

the liturgy for discernment

people to show up on the first Saturday night of each month to serve and listen to these youth. We need everyone to participate. God is not finished with this church yet. We have a ministry to do. We have young people to welcome."

A few months later James sent me a copy of a flyer that he and the youth ministry team had posted in motel break rooms, lift-operator stations, and fast-food restaurants where young people gathered. The poster had a picture of a warm, friendly grandmother working over a hot stove and it read, "Grandma's Home Cooking. Fresh-made soup. Home-baked cookies. Free shoes, jackets, and pants. A listening ear. Everyone's welcome. First Saturday of each month. St. John's Episcopal Church." Sixty youth showed up the next month and the month after that. Some of the young people began to inquire about the symbols in the sanctuary. Others asked if they could come to worship.

What's remarkable about this story is that James and the youth ministry team followed God's timing. They had the trust and patience to spend a year meeting for prayer, sharing, and deep listening before discerning God's leading. When they finally began a youth ministry, it looked very different from anything they'd expected, and was a much more natural fit with their gifts than if they had tried to emulate the ministries of other churches.

The liturgy for discernment is just one way in which God's presence and guidance can be made central to our ministries. There are many other ways in which a youth ministry might become more transparent to God's life and calling. Whatever the method, my experience has been that as churches gather on behalf of young people in prayer, relationship, and trust, a ministry begins to emerge that is organic and life-giving to both youth and adults. Over time, relationships begin to develop, and the cultural divide between youth and adults begins to dissipate. It becomes unclear who is giving and who is receiving. The youth ministry becomes a setting in which youth and adults grow together in their life with God.

# noticing

# 11

I think the most powerful aspect of contemplative youth ministry has been giving young people the space and opportunity to notice God in their lives. Creating exercises where kids can notice God invites a sense of wonder. Simply asking, "What did you notice?" has caused senior high students, junior high students, Sunday school teachers, congregational members, and myself to "see God" in our ordinary days. As I've asked kids to tell me where they encounter God in worship, I've heard all kinds of wonderful responses: "When I lit the candles." "In the stained-glass windows." "In my father's eyes during the sermon." "In the sharing of the peace." "In the sound of my own voice saying the Lord's Prayer."

—CHRIS BERTHELSEN, PASTOR, FIRST LUTHERAN CHURCH, ST. PAUL, MINNESOTA

I mean, teens nowadays are so busy and so stressed out, that it's kind of hard to imagine them ever sitting still contemplating and noticing God in their lives, but it really does work. It just came naturally and more naturally than I'd ever, you know, thought. And I've taken it home. My mom knows that if I'm up at six in the morning and there's a little sticky note on my door that she shouldn't come in, it's because I'm usually sitting there in silence praying. And I know my parents notice a difference in the way I act toward others. After I've had that time to just be silent and

contemplative youth ministry

I guess be held by God, there's a difference, you know—how I talk to others, my reaction time, what I get offended by is completely changed when I've already taken that time to be within myself and then respond to other people.

There's a quote I heard from one of the spiritual directors at a youth event. It's from St. Seraphim. He said, "If you alone find God, thousands around you will be saved." And that's very true in contemplative prayer. I really believe it's about the way you treat others after you come inside yourself and see what's important and what's in your heart and how God's speaking to you. There's a complete difference.

—LAUREN, AGE 16, CLEVELAND, OHIO

Most of this book has focused on the disposition and practice of adults in youth ministry. This is important because adults hold the power and set the climate for spiritual formation. As Gina Yeager, the director of youth ministry for the Presbyterian Church USA, once said to me, "Youth ministry is just as much about adults as it is youth." Yet the question remains: What do we do with the kids? How does a contemplative attitude affect our ministry with youth?

Young people need adults who have gained wisdom through their personal experience of God. But our desire for young people isn't just that they'll be surrounded by adults who know God; it goes deeper than that. Our desire is that youth will begin to recognize and experience God's presence for themselves. This is the hope: that more and more young people will begin to see, hear, know, and nurture God's

noticing

presence in the intimacies of their lives and their interactions with the larger world.

Our first task as youth ministers is to be with young people just as Jesus was with people. Our second task is to help youth develop the eyes, ears, and heart of Jesus for themselves. We're not only called to be witnesses among young people, we are also called, like Jesus, to be teachers. We're called to awaken youth to the presence of God in the world.

Much of my understanding and practice of youth ministry comes from my experience in spiritual direction. Spiritual directors are people who have the gift of spiritual friendship. They seek to be present and attentive to others. They listen and look for signs of God in the experiences of others. Spiritual directors aren't experts on God; in fact, good spiritual directors are very aware of their ignorance, blindness, and limitations in regards to the spiritual lives of others. They trust that God is doing the ministry, so they are satisfied to stand on the sidelines of a person's life and simply reflect what they are seeing.

Author and Episcopal priest Alan Jones tells the story of the first person who came to him for spiritual direction. Alan was young—just out of seminary and still unsure of his vocation. An elderly monk who was a renowned scholar and a deep man of prayer, considered a saint by his community, came to Alan and said, "Alan, I want you to be my spiritual director."

"But brother, I can't!" Alan pleaded.

With a twinkle in his eye, the wise monk responded: "I know!"[22]

The older teacher knew that the real director was the Holy Spirit, not Alan, and that Alan would do fine as a spiritual director as long as he didn't rely on his own skills. As youth ministers we seek the same humility. We trust that God is the real director of young people's

[22] *Exploring Spiritual Direction: An Essay on Christian Friendship* (Seabury Press, 1982), 8

contemplative youth ministry

souls. Our role is to notice, to point, to help when asked, and to avoid relying too heavily on our own skills and learning.

Elizabeth Liebert, professor of spiritual life at San Francisco Theological Seminary, describes the movements within a spiritual direction relationship. These movements are *noticing, naming*, and *nurturing*. Noticing refers to the way in which we help people (through careful attentiveness) become more aware of their experience of God. Naming involves aiding people in finding language and theology for their experience. And finally, nurturing concerns the ways we help people develop practices and disciplines that deepen their relationship with God.

In the next three chapters, I will explore this triptych and reveal how we might help young people respond to Jesus' invitation to freedom. This chapter will focus on noticing—helping youth become aware of their experience of God. The two chapters that follow will explore "naming" (helping youth find words for the experience of God) and "nurturing" (helping youth develop practices that deepen their understanding and relationship with God).

## Noticing

The human heart, be it young or old, longs to experience the presence of God. Religious words and symbols, no matter how inspiring, are not enough. We all desire to know God for ourselves. "Don't just tell me about Jesus," young people seem to say. "Let me meet Jesus for myself."

As we seek to become contemplative ministers, we not only strive to deepen our own awareness of God within our ministries, but we also seek to help *young people* open their eyes and ears to the movement of God. One way we do this is by noticing. Knowing God is present and at work within all of our young people, we attend to them like watchmen anticipating the morning. We wait patiently, seeking to become aware of the ways in which Jesus is courting our youth. We invite young people to see for themselves. We encourage them to look for God, to listen for God, to reach out and seek God with all their heart, mind, soul, and strength. We tell them, "Don't take my word for it. Go ahead. Taste and see that the Lord is good."

In order to help young people notice God, we must trust that all teenagers know something of God. If we trust God is present with us in the world, then we know all young people have some experience of God. These experiences are like seeds that need to be identified, nurtured, and tended until they bloom. Our first task as youth ministers is simply to help young people notice their experiences of God. Unfortunately, most young people have gone through some sort of spiritual "deformation." They've been taught that God exists only in the Bible, in ancient times, or in other "holier" people. Conventional, word-heavy Christian education programs give the impression that God is distant, abstract, a reality only for ministers and the religiously trained. More charismatic youth ministries can give the equally false assumption that God is present only in the spectacular—miraculous healings, powerful speakers, mystical saints, and life-changing testimonies.

Unfortunately, what's rarely communicated to youth is that the experience of God is actually quite ordinary and even common. Jesus claims to be present whenever two or three are gathered in his name. "God is love," we're told in 1 John—intimating that God is present in every true experience of love. Paul writes that moments of joy, patience, and kindness are experiences of the Holy Spirit. People in the New Testament encountered Jesus while working, eating, praying, conversing, traveling, and engaging in other ordinary human experiences. As youth ministers we don't need to convince young people of the presence of God. We don't need to "deliver" God to young people. We simply need to help young people notice the ways in which each and every one of them is already in relationship with God. Our role is to help youth recognize the ways in which Jesus is already near, already seeking trust and friendship.

How do we help young people notice their experience of God?

## 1. We point.

More ministers need to take their cues from John the Baptist. Not only did John open his eyes and ears to the presence of God, he also sought to help others notice God. John was a pointer. When John sees Jesus coming to be baptized, he singles him out to his followers and says, "Here is the Lamb of God" (John 1:29). One of the first ways we can help youth become more aware of their life in God is to point to the moments when Jesus seems near. We notice when young people are alive, when their hearts are "burning" within them (see Luke 24:32). We notice when they seem open to God. We notice when youth are living like Jesus. We notice when the fruits of the Spirit are present in them—when they're giving or receiving love, joy, peace, patience, kindness, generosity, faithfulness, and gentleness. We hold up these moments to young people until they notice them for themselves—until they see that they are in the stream of God's love, that they are participating in Jesus' way of life.

For seven years I took youth groups from Oregon and California on week-long house-building projects among the shanty towns that exist just across the U.S. border in Mexico. These trips were transformative for both youth and adults, as we sought to live in community with Mexican citizens, many of whom were struggling to find work in the border factories that provide cheap goods for U.S. consumers.

On one particular trip, I spent a few days working with a group of teens from a U.S. suburb who were deeply motivated to build a home for a Mexican family that included a mother, father, grandmother, and four small children. The group arrived early to the worksite eager

noticing

to get started. The appreciative mother and grandmother sat on fruit crates smiling and grateful at the prospect of a new home while the children ran around the work site enamored by the teenagers with their tool belts and baseball caps. During our first lunch break, the children were eager to interact with our group. They stood by, wide-eyed, as we took out sack lunches filled with stuffed deli sandwiches, juice drinks, fruit, and cookies. One teenage girl, Clare, noticed the disparity between her lunch and the few lime-sprinkled tortillas the children were sharing. She gestured discreetly for the children to come sit by her. I watched as she carefully divided her lunch, giving equal parts to each of the four children, who received the gifts with grateful smiles and ate giggling with glee.

As the teens went back to work, I noticed that the oldest of the four, a boy about nine years of age, took off running to a field at the edge of the makeshift community. A few minutes later he returned, holding a small bouquet of yellow flowers. He stood shyly at the edge of the worksite, watching as Clare crouched on her hands and knees spreading cement. I went back to work, but from time to time I noticed the boy, sometimes standing, sometimes sitting, holding his small cluster of flowers and waiting to catch Clare's attention. We finished the foundation and soon were deep in mud and water, rinsing and cleaning our tools. Clare finished up and jumped into the back of our work truck. I watched as the boy followed her and stood by the back of the truck, now holding a tired and wilting bunch of flowers. He called over the side of the truck, *"Señorita, Señorita."* Clare was busy chatting with her friends and comparing scratches and bruises from a hard day of work. She was unaware of the boy. One of our adult leaders jumped in the cab of the truck and soon Clare, her friends, and the bed of tools were bouncing back to our campsite.

The next day another youth group at a different site requested additional workers. Clare volunteered to leave her own youth group to assist there. For the next three days, she built walls, nailed roofing material, and spread stucco with teenagers at the site. Finally, on the last day of our trip, Clare returned to her friends and the original worksite with the four children. Clare was excited to see her friends and immediately became immersed in conversation. She talked and worked with her two best buddies so intensely that she hardly noticed the nine-year-old boy following her throughout her activities. I noticed, however, that from time to time the boy would call to her saying, "Señorita, Señorita." A few times Clare heard the boy and smiled or patted his head, but continued to work and talk with her friends. As the day came to a close, so did our work on the house. The roof and walls were complete, prompting the group to give a great cheer. The family was brought together in front of the simple dwelling and presented with gifts—blankets, food, and toys for the kids. I noticed again as the oldest boy moved closer to Clare, tugging on her shirt. She turned and gave him a quick and somewhat perfunctory hug, then returned to chatting excitedly with her friends while the boy stood, once again, waiting for her attention.

After a prayer and many hugs, we all ran for the vans hoping to beat the descending darkness. I counted the kids to make sure no one was left behind, grabbed a seat, shut the door, and then took one last look at the worksite. I spied a sweatshirt that someone had left behind. I asked the driver to wait as I stepped out of the car and ran to get the shirt. As I returned to the vehicle, I noticed the same boy who'd spent the day seeking Clare's attention. He was standing at the rear of the van, crying and looking up through the back window where Clare was seated. Remembering how persistently he'd sought Clare's attention, I went to the van, asked the driver to turn off the engine, and asked Clare to step out and go see the boy. She was startled at first, but made her way through her friends, climbed out of the van, walked over to the boy, and, for the first time since their lunch together, knelt down and gave him her full attention.

noticing

The boy smiled at her with wet eyes, then reached into his back pocket, took out a small handful of crushed yellow flowers, and offered them to her. Clare looked at the crumpled offering quizzically at first, but then realized what was taking place. *"Para la comida"* ("For the food"), he said. Clare carefully brushed the flowers from his hand into hers, wrapped her fingers around the tender gift, closed her eyes, and held it to her heart. The boy smiled with relief. Then he wrapped his arms around her neck and pressed his cheek against hers. He hung there for a long moment, then he stepped away, walked back to his family, turned, and waved.

In my life as a minister, there have been a few precious moments when I've had the privilege to witness a young person's heart break open to the mystery of God's love. This was one of them. I watched as Clare looked at that boy. I watched as she looked down at the frail gift in her hands. I watched as she climbed back into the van, holding the present she'd received, and then gazed back through the window at the boy and his family. And I knew, just as she knew, that she would no longer be the same.

By pointing out the crying boy to Clare, I was able to point to the way in which the Holy Spirit was present. Pulling Clare from the energy of her friends, I helped her notice the way God's grace was pursuing her. Had I not stopped the van driver and asked Clare to be with the boy, she might never have received the gift of the boy's gratitude. She might have forgotten her own act of generosity and kindness. She might have missed the way she was participating in God's work of love. Just as Jesus tells people again and again, "Your faith has made you well," we seek to point out the moments when teenagers are living in faith, sometimes even before they've claimed it for themselves. We pay attention to the moments when their hearts are open and then we point and say, "You seem to really care about those people." We say, "You seem more yourself—why is that?" We reflect, "You're so alive today." We then offer, "Here is the Lamb of

God." "This is the Christian life." "This is the experience of God the Bible speaks of. God is here. The kingdom of God is within you. You're living like Jesus. Can you see it?"

## 2. We question.

Another way we help young people notice God is by simply asking them, "How is God present?" I ask this question when kids are at play, when they're with their friends, when they reflect on their home situations or future vocations. Like a good spiritual director I want to continually invite young people to reflect on God's presence within their experiences: "How is God present? Where do you notice God? How is Jesus among us?"

When I ask young people to turn their attention to the presence of God, a number of things take place. First, I'm reminding them that God is present and available. This is especially powerful if I ask the question while they talk about a school situation, a moment of pain or suffering, or a seemingly mundane experience. When I ask them to notice God, I'm communicating the possibility that each and every moment of our lives is alive with the presence of God. Second, the question also communicates that youth have the capacity to notice God. There is a sense of empowerment as I invite them to be "religious interpreters"—people who can perceive and become aware of the movement of God. Third, I'm helping them reflect on their real-life theologies and religious biases. When I ask a young person, "How is God present in this moment?" she may respond, "I don't think God has anything to do with my school; God is just about praying and church." To ask youth to notice God is to invite them to reflect on their beliefs concerning God's relationship to the world. Finally, when I ask young people to notice the Holy Spirit in their midst, I'm helping them develop their sensitivity to God. They have to pause, become aware of what they're seeing, hearing, feeling, and thinking.

noticing

By asking young people how God is present, we invite them to reflect as full conversation partners in the Christian faith. The Bible was written by people who asked themselves how God was present in their experiences and then wrote down what they noticed. When youth are allowed to reflect on this question, they are given respect as full conversation partners.

When I was working as a youth minister in Portland, Oregon, there was a group of girls who would cut class in the middle of the day and gather on a downtown corner to smoke cigarettes. Over time I befriended them. One day they asked about my job as a minister. I responded with something like, "I'm trying to help people become aware of God's presence in their lives and in the world."

"Well, I can tell you God isn't in my life," said one young woman, whom I later learned had been abused and abandoned by her father.

We talked for a while, and then I asked if they would try an experiment with me. I asked them to move back from the curb and stand against the outside wall of a coffee shop, observing the sights around them. I invited them to look at the cars and the people, the trees across the street, the buildings, and the cloud formations in the sky. "Just for a moment, allow yourself to believe in God," I said. "Just suspend your doubt for a moment and imagine that God is present in the world. Then reflect on how God would be here, in this moment." For about five minutes the girls stood, taking in the activity around them. I asked them what they noticed.

"God would be in that sleeping drunk across the street, waiting for someone to give him a place to sleep."

"I think God would be in the sound of the birds singing in those trees. I don't know if anyone notices, but I do every time I'm down here—and it makes me peaceful."

On and on they went, noticing the God they didn't believe in. And then the girl who'd been abandoned by her father said, "If God exists, he would be in the seeds of the grass that are still waiting for the sunlight, waiting to grow, underneath the pavement and cement."

For the next six months, I met with this group of young women. Each week we'd talk, drink coffee, and then I'd ask the question, "Where is God in this moment?" Together we'd respond and reflect. They'd listen to me. I would listen to them. Eventually, a few of them began attending our church youth group and became followers of Jesus. But the girl who'd been abandoned slowly disappeared into the streets.

A number of years later, I ran into one of the street-corner smokers. I asked about her friend who'd been abandoned by her father. She told me she'd become addicted to heroin, then contracted AIDS and disappeared from the area. I was shocked. I felt deeply saddened by the news and grieved over not doing more to reach out to her. She was right, I thought, God was in the grass seeds—her own fading hope, underneath the black pavement, waiting for the sun.

## 3. We Invite.

Another powerful way in which young people notice their relationship with God is through prayer—listening forms of prayer that make space for youth to encounter God directly. Every time I lead a Sunday school class or youth group meeting, I try to create a setting where young people can explore their experience and relationship with God. Traditional forms of youth ministry are often word-heavy, placing the teacher as the sole mediator of God. The teacher talks about God, the teacher leads the discussion about God, and then the teacher closes in prayer. In this model, a young person's relationship with the Holy is only through the teacher. As long as the teacher is approachable and trustworthy, the young people are willing to listen; however, there comes a point when the words of faith become empty if youth aren't given the opportunity to experience the God behind the teaching.

noticing

There are many ways in which we can invite young people to notice God directly in their experience. Many books contain prayer exercises that can be used with youth.[23] Here are a few exercises I've found particularly helpful:

- *Creative Prayer.* Clay, crayons, paints, and paper—all of these materials can help facilitate a young person's awareness of God. They are especially helpful for younger teens, who often find silent prayer abstract and uncomfortable. Sometimes I use these materials with very open instructions. I ask young people to take some paper and a handful of crayons. I invite them to find a space where they can pray. I invite them to turn to God in prayer and say something like, "God, how are you present in my life at this time?" I instruct them to wait in silence until they feel ready to express what they notice through the colors and paper. I remind them this isn't an art exercise. There's no grade, no expectation as to how their image might unfold. I tell them they may find that a single color expresses their experience of God and spend the time scribbling with that particular color, or they might have a particular image that seems important and spend the prayer time exploring that image. I give the youth 15 or 20 minutes to pray with the colors (or clay or other creative medium), then I ask them to come together and share what they noticed. "How was God with you in this prayer? What did you notice about your relationship with God in this exercise?"

    Sometimes I offer more direct instructions. I say, "Pray with the colors, asking Jesus to show you the ways in which he is grateful for you." Or, "As you pray with the clay, ask how God is present within the problems or suffering you face in your life." I've found exercises with art media to be particularly powerful when led with a sense of both prayer and playfulness.

contemplative youth ministry

---

[23] Works on prayer such as Daniel Wolpert's *Creating a Life with God*, Tilden Edwards's *Living in the Presence*, Marjorie Thompson's *Soul Feast*, and Tony Jones's *Soul Shaper* (written specifically for youth ministers) all contain exercises and prayers that can be helpful in awakening young people to the love of God.

- *Walking Prayer.* Prayers that give youth permission to use their bodies are more likely to engage them than standard prayers. One of the spiritual exercises I've found most helpful is to invite youth to take a walk with Jesus. After a few moments of silence, I invite them to go outside and then, in their own way, ask Jesus to walk with them. I ask them to refrain from interacting with others, but instead, to take their time strolling around the neighborhood, noticing the sights and sounds that catch their attention. I tell them to spend extra time with anything that seems to stand out or grab their interest.

Sometimes, when working with kids who are still very skeptical, I'll say something like, "As you go on your walk, say the following prayer: 'God, if you exist, help me notice you during this time.'" I give kids about 15 minutes to walk, and then have them gather back together in silence. After everyone has returned, I ask the kids to share their experiences.

I remember working with a youth group that had two "skater" boys who were forced to attend church and resisted all forms of spiritual reflection. I invited them to take a prayer walk as an experiment—to see if they would notice God's presence while they meandered through the surrounding neighborhood. Surprisingly, they did the exercise. When they returned, I asked them what they noticed. One of the skater boys raised his hand and shared, "I immediately walked to the street where I like to skateboard. I walked slowly and prayed just as you told us to. For some reason, as I was walking I felt like I should look up. When I did, I noticed these incredible tree branches reaching out from both sides of the street, covering the street like a canopy. The leaves were red and orange, filtering the sun. I lay down on my back on the sidewalk and just looked at these trees. I couldn't believe I'd never noticed them before. It was like they were these big arms, covering the street, protecting the place where I skate. I was so amazed. I just kept saying, 'Is this you, God? Is this you?'"

Walking prayers can be used after Bible studies or lesson times to give young people a chance to reflect on the material with God. For example, after a lesson on service, youth can be invited to take a prayer walk, asking God to help them reflect on how God is drawing them to serve. Or after studying the prodigal son, or the grateful leper, youth can be asked to take a prayerful walk, asking God to reflect with them on their experience of gratitude or repentance.

- *The Awareness Examen.* Ignatius' examination of conscience (see chapter 8) is a simple way to help young people notice their experience of God. I've used the examen at the beginning of Sunday school classes, in youth meetings, mission trips, meal times, and even informal get-togethers with youth. The examen gives them the opportunity to catch their breath, savor their experience, and notice how God is present in their lives. I invite youth to look over their day and ask God to bring to them all the moments of grace (or sometimes I replace "grace" with "gratitude" or "love"[24]). I invite them to choose one of those moments to reflect on in the silence: "How is God present in this experience? What is God's invitation to you in this experience?" I give them a few moments to rest in gratitude for whatever moment has come to their attention. Then I invite them to share their experiences with the group.

One time the youth in my church decided to practice the examen each night during the 40 days of Lent. An adult from the church paired up with each young person, and the pair spoke every night and practiced the prayer over the phone. After Easter we held an all-church retreat where some of the youth and adults shared their experiences. Of particular interest to me was the fact that the partcipants, young and old,

[24] See *Sleeping with Bread* by Dennis LInn, Sheila Fabricant Linn and Matthew Linn.

contemplative youth ministry

found that they began to experience great transformation through this simple exercise. As the pairs practiced the examen, they became more mindful of God's presence during their days. They found themselves seeking to live more fully into the places and experiences where they'd noticed God's grace, and seeking to move through the moments where they'd noticed resistance to God's love. They found their daily lives more imbued with a sense of God's love and presence.

- *Silent Prayer.* When I meet with young people in a youth group or Sunday school setting, I often engage them in Bible study on a particular subject, story, or parable. After we've spent some time discussing a particular Scripture passage, I then invite them to turn their attention to God. I ask them to allow themselves to be with God directly in the midst of whatever content we've explored. If we're reading the Psalms and discussing suffering, I light a candle at the close of the discussion and ask the youth to close their eyes and simply rest with God beneath all we've discussed. We allow the words to settle. I then invite them to pray in the silence, "God, how have you been present in this discussion? What do you seek to teach us?" After a few minutes of silence, I invite kids to share. In this way, we make space for God—space for young people to engage God directly in the midst of our conversation and learning. In the Quaker tradition, people sometimes call for silence in the midst of a meeting. The call for silence is an invitation to stop, turn to God, and listen. I try to call for silence in the midst of work projects, lessons, play time, and conversation. The call to stop and listen—even if it's just for 30 seconds—is another opportunity for young people to turn and notice God within their experiences.

I try to incorporate silence into every youth event and meeting. Over time, I have found that these times of quiet become more and more attractive to young people. Recently, while leading a week-long youth camp, I invited kids to spend a whole afternoon in silent prayer. After a few words about the silent prayer tradition, I sent them out along a deserted coastline to pray and be with God in silent communion. At the end of our event, I asked kids to rate their most significant experiences of the week. I was shocked to find that the majority of kids listed the silent time on the coast as their favorite experience—even when compared to day-trips to San Francisco, recreational games, and free time with friends.

- *Contemplative Prayer.* Classical forms of contemplative prayer such as *lectio divina*, Ignatian contemplation, and even centering prayer can be incredibly fruitful for young people in helping them deepen their awareness of God. A friend who serves in a United Methodist church practices *lectio divina* with the youth in her confirmation program. She's found that at the end of the year, kids continually cite *lectio divina* as the most significant part of the class.

  It's reasonable to offer some modifications when leading these prayers with youth. Remember that kids, like adults, live in a multitasking, attention-demanding culture that presents them with a barrage of sights, sounds, and temptations. Silence and prayer can be incredibly difficult. Make sure to keep an informal attitude when inviting youth into silence. Add some humor. The more you try to make the prayer pristine and "spiritual," the more uncomfortable the kids feel, and they'll start giggling. Acknowledge that it might feel awkward. Use an experimental tone. Say things like, "I know this may seem strange, but let's try this as an experiment. We're going to take three minutes of silence to spend time resting in God. You may find your mind wandering. You may feel like fidgeting. All of that's okay—we're just seeing what it's like to rest and be with God."

Make sure you use very short periods of silence when you first expose kids to contemplative prayer. Even 30 seconds can seem like a long time. I once led a junior high group where we spent a month pausing for only 10 to 15 seconds of silence. After a year the kids could handle about 30 seconds. A year later we spent almost five minutes in silence each time we met. It takes time to get used to just being with God.

The environment can be a help or hindrance when leading kids in contemplative prayer. Set a mood that's conducive to silence. Turn out the lights and light a candle. Go outside under the stars. Play some music that helps youth settle down. Make sure there's plenty of space. Better yet, ask the youth to set up the room for contemplative prayer. I find that youth are very receptive to contemplative prayer, especially when led by adults who are experienced in prayer and can lead it with a sense of "lightness."

A note of caution: It can be incredibly painful and even destructive for kids to be led into contemplative prayer or a spiritual exercise by people who have little experience. I've had too many painful experiences of watching adults who had little experience in contemplative prayer try to lead kids in such exercises. Often, adults set high expectations, creating a heavy atmosphere where kids feel obligated to produce an experience of God. In the appendix at the end of this book, you'll find a guideline for leading a prayer exercise with youth. I urge you to use this guideline—it has been refined over the years by many youth workers as they have sought to help kids pray contemplatively.

Of course, the best way to learn how to lead kids in prayer is to spend time in prayer. Go on prayer retreats, read books on prayer, and most importantly spend time in prayer yourself. As you cultivate your own life of prayer, you'll learn

noticing

more about how to help kids pray and how to respond when they face difficulties in their own prayer lives.

## 4. We Create Circumstances.

"It is circumstances, not ideas, that change people," author and Catholic priest Richard Rohr once said.[25] Possibly the most significant way we can help youth notice their experience of God is by helping them engage in real life. It's amazing how much time young people spend in "virtual life." I'm not just talking about the time spent in front of televisions, computers, and video devices (where statistics say most teens spend more than 24 hours a week!). I'm also referring to school, where most youth spend the majority of their daylight hours. Kids often feel the message they receive in school, in church, and in their own families is that life begins after college. Or that it begins once they're married and have a good job. There's a sense that the time spent in school and church isn't "real life," but simply preparation for real life. It's a great disservice to young people if our youth ministry programs communicate the same message.

We can help young people notice the presence of God by helping them see that their lives have already begun, that their decisions matter, that their lives have meaning and can help bring care and change into the world right now. This is why it's important to get kids out of the youth room or Sunday school class and into the streets. It's important to take kids on trips where they meet new and different kinds of people. It's important to give them situations where they can work and serve and make a difference. Then, in these real life settings, ask them, "How is God present here?" I ask youth to notice how they feel—scared, frightened, sad, happy—and then ask them how God might be within those feelings.

I've always felt it was my responsibility to invite young people to have their hearts broken by the things that break Jesus' heart. Just as

contemplative youth ministry

[25] In March, 1990 during a series of talks and discussions in Germany, some of which are recorded in *Simplicity: The Art of Living* (Crossroad, 1991).

196

Jesus enters into the lives of suffering people, so too have I tried to invite young people into the suffering places of humanity. Jesus tells us these places of suffering are places where he is most available. I want kids to listen to people who've suffered tragedy and hardship. I want them to befriend people who spend their days seeking food and clean water. I want them to experience some of the hopelessness that exists in this world, so they can make contact with the suffering of God, so they can sense the compassion of Jesus, and so they can feel God calling them to be a source of life and healing in this world.

A few years ago I helped lead a week-long contemplative retreat with high school students. We began each day with a morning prayer service that involved silence and contemplative prayer. Throughout the day we told kids stories of different contemplative saints within the Christian tradition and led them through various prayer exercises. On the fourth day of the retreat, we decided to take the youth out of the chapel and into the streets. We took them to a Franciscan community in the Tenderloin district of San Francisco that provides lunch to over 2,500 homeless people each day. We showed up to help serve in the kitchen. But when one of the brothers in the community met us, he told us it would be much more significant to simply spend some time eating and visiting with people. We dispersed the youth throughout the serpentine line of hungry people. They waited for a half hour or so, shuffling up to the front door of the building toward the kitchen. The youth introduced themselves to the folks in line and spent the lunchtime eating and conversing. For the rest of the afternoon, we hung out on the street listening to people's stories, then ended the day in St. Basil's Chapel, where many of the homeless in that area gather to rest and pray.

On our way home, one young girl from Omaha, Nebraska, told me she would soon graduate from high school and had planned to become a hairdresser. She revealed, however, that after spending time with folks in the city, she had made a commitment to God to become

noticing

197

a teacher and serve people like the ones she'd met in the Tenderloin district. I thought it was a beautiful dream, but didn't know how much weight to give it. Four years later I received a letter from the youth worker in this young girl's parish. In the letter he told me that the young woman who had spent that day in the Tenderloin district had nearly completed her teaching certificate and was looking for a job in one of the poorer neighborhoods of Omaha. I've had countless similar experiences in which young people, placed within the center of human life and struggle, hear God's love and call.

## Slow Club

My son Joseph is a natural contemplative. When he was four years old, he was no longer willing to be hustled to preschool and hurried along on errands. One morning Joseph announced he was starting a new organization called "Slow Club," in which he would serve as president. The rules of the club were simple: No running and no hurrying. Unfortunately, neither his parents nor his brother could commit to these regulations, so for the next year Joseph was the only member of his club. Each morning, he'd stroll to school at his natural pace. If I tried to pull him along or anxiously urge him to "hurry it up!" he'd respond calmly, "I'm president of Slow Club, Dad. I don't hurry."

At night over dinner, Joseph would talk about his club. He told us about the things he noticed during the day and shook his head at the other children who always seemed too busy to see the marvels and treasures so clearly visible to the patient eye: a piece of wire, a bottle cap, an especially smooth rock, a line of ants. From time to time he'd invite neighbors or other friends to join his organization, but no one could commit to his charter.

One summer while I was teaching at a youth camp, Joseph granted me a one-day membership to his club. After playing ultimate Frisbee with a group of teenagers, the bell rang for lunch. The kids bolted toward the dining hall. Joseph had been watching the game, so I ran over to him, put on my sweatshirt, grabbed his hand, and began pulling him hastily behind the group. I was hungry and wanted to get a place in line. Joseph reminded me, however, that I'd accepted his one-day club membership and would need to reduce my speed drastically. I took a deep breath and reluctantly slowed to my son's pace. Joseph looked at me satisfied, and then said, "You see, Dad, when you slow down, you notice things. Just look around as we walk, and you'll see things everyone else has missed."

Quietly we strolled through the campground, looking carefully at our surroundings. Suddenly, I saw something move off to the side of the path. "Joseph!" I whispered excitedly. "Look over there." He turned, and we both saw two jackrabbits standing on their hind legs, watching us. Joseph gave me a knowing smile and said, "I bet we're the only ones who noticed those rabbits." We walked on, stopping to look at butterflies, strange purple wildflowers, enormous beetles, and a lizard with half a tail. When we joined the rest of the family, we both talked excitedly about the treasures we'd seen.

Like Joseph, those of us who minister among young people seek to be members of Slow Club. We invite youth to attend to their lives; we encourage them not to overlook the signs of God's presence. Every time we're among youth, we look and listen with slow eyes and ears. We listen for the deep sounds of God. We look patiently for the little signs of grace. We cultivate wonder. Like Joseph, we walk beside them saying, "What do you notice? What do you see? How is God present in this moment?"

I want to be a member of Slow Club. I want to be a still and knowing presence among young people. I want to walk beside them, stopping from time to time to notice the God who waits to be received.

noticing

naming

12

Although I didn't realize it at the time, my interaction with our teens was more about conveying a quick burst of information (Hi. How are you? Great, now let me tell you what you need to know...) and less about actually listening. My relationship with our teens was pretty superficial. As I was introduced to and started to regularly practice contemplative prayer, I found myself slowing down in a variety of ways. With my youth that meant not asking a question until I was ready to really listen to the answer. It also meant not being anxious to move on to the next teen, but instead to be comfortable listening to the teen's responses, however long they took. I also noticed I was much more likely to ask some follow-up questions to get a deeper understanding of what was happening in their lives. My transformation allows me to start from a point of deeper interest and slowly bring them into a deeper relationship with me as we collectively enter into a deeper relationship with Christ.

—JOHN FREY, BUSINESS EXECUTIVE, YOUTH MINISTRY VOLUNTEER, DISCIPLES OF CHRIST, HOUSTON, TEXAS

But who do you say that I am?

—MATTHEW 16:15

The Bible was written by people who encountered the mystery of God. The authors of the New Testament sought to put into words the overwhelming experience of the mystery of God that they had in Jesus Christ. This is the same pattern of spiritual growth we seek to facilitate among young people. We want them to meet and experience the God Jesus sought to reveal. We do this by creating settings and situations, time and space for youth to notice God's presence and love. The next step is to help them find words for their experience. An experience of God that isn't named or marked in some way is often lost or ignored. We need words or symbols for our experience of God in order to hold and savor the ways God is with us. In youth ministry we seek to help young people locate their experience of God within the language and experience of the Christian tradition, and then nurture their experience (their relationship with God) through practices of living that keep them available to God and others.

Possibly the most important skill in ministering with youth is knowing when to talk and when to listen. I've leaned heavily in this book on the importance of presence—being present not only to young people, but also to the God who moves within and among young people. I emphasize the importance of presence and listening because most teenagers experience adults as either absent or lecturing. Being a listening presence to youth and God are foundational skills in ministry—and often ignored in most youth curricula. However, I don't want to ignore the importance of speaking, of words. Adolescent spiritual formation means not only helping youth recognize God, but helping them name this God as well. Good teaching is as important as good listening. It's just that good teaching, especially spiritual teaching, always begins with listening, with noticing, with waiting, with prayer and presence. It's out of our presence to young people and God that we're given words to speak and teach.

There are myriad books written about good teaching techniques, but here are some of the primary ways in which I seek to help youth find words for their experiences of God:

## 1. Who do you say that I am?

It's interesting how many books and curriculum programs try to explain Jesus to young people. Language is important. Theology is important. But these attempts to describe and define Jesus are quite different from Jesus' own teaching style. Jesus is careful not to say too much about who he is. He uses strange terms like "the Son of Man." He speaks often of "the Father," but says very little about his own identity. When he does speak of himself, he talks in parables and poetic language, referencing things like bread, light, water, and vines. "Who do you say I am?" is the primary question he brings to Peter, and the question he seems to bring to all of us. "Jesus is the question, not the answer," C.S. Lewis once wrote. Jesus relies on our experience, our encounters with him first, and then out of this he asks us, "Who do you say that I am?"

When I work with youth, I try to be mindful of Jesus' teaching style. I try not to say too much. I try to create space, prayer exercises, and service opportunities and then ask them, "Who do you say God is?" I try to help them lean into Jesus' life and then ask them to give me words for their experience. I hand out journals to write in. I sit them in circles and invite them to speak. I ask, "Who is this God you experience?" or "Who is this God you don't experience?" I question them, "Who is Jesus?" "How are you like Jesus?" "How are you different from Jesus?" It's important for young people to speak the real words that express their understanding and experience of God. This is true dialogue: to give space not only for youth to listen, but also for youth to speak.

It was only my second Sunday as a volunteer when I asked the one question you don't ask in a junior high Sunday school room: "If

Jesus were here, do you think he would attend this church?" A hand shot up. It was Sam, the wary eighth-grade boy who rarely spoke. "Of course not," he barked, surprising everyone. "Jesus would be bored here. He'd rather be out doing something. I never read in the Bible that he went to church. If he were here, he'd be helping people or checking out nature—that's what he did in the Bible. You'd never find Jesus sitting through all these long boring church services."

The rest of the class sat silent in anticipation, basking in the awkward moment. I had the feeling I'd just crossed a line. The regular teacher gave me a sharp look that said, "Thanks for undermining a year's worth of work!" Then she turned to Sam and said, "You know, Sam, I think a lot of people in this church would be really hurt to hear you say that. Everyone at this church works really hard. If they heard you say that Jesus wouldn't come here, I think they would feel devastated."

Sam looked down, embarrassed, unsure of how to respond to this shaming. The other youth looked down as well. One mature 13-year-old girl attempted to rescue us. "I think Jesus would like to come to our church and listen to the sermons, since they're always about him," she offered. Sam rolled his eyes and then slung his head down, avoiding eye contact with the leaders. In a soft, steady voice he asked, "What kind of egomaniac wants to come and hear people talk about how great he is? Is Jesus really that insecure?"

The leader went on the defensive. She spent the next 20 minutes explaining to Sam (and to herself?) the purpose of worship services, church institutions, and life on planet earth. Our ears full, we were all grateful when the class time ended. I walked out with Sam. "So be more specific," I said, ignoring the past 20 minutes. "If Jesus were in this town, where do you think he'd go?"

Sam picked up the conversation instantly: "Wherever there is life. You know, wherever there's the opposite of boring."

naming

"What do you mean 'the opposite of boring'?"

"You know, boring is like when you really don't need to be there, when it doesn't matter if you're there or not. Boring is the opposite of living. Jesus would be wherever people are really living, whether it's sad or happy—anything that's not, you know, like...flat."

Curious, I stopped, turned to Sam, and smiled. "The way I see it," he continued thoughtfully, "Jesus was all about life. Doesn't he say somewhere that, 'I am life...' or something?"

"So where do you find life?" I asked.

"That's easy—at the beach. If my mom wanted me to be close to God, she should take me surfing each Sunday." He paused and smiled. He liked this idea. "You know, you could make the whole thing a different kind of church. We could pray or something, read Scripture—you know, make it spiritual, and then we could go out and surf with Jesus. It could be like prayer. No talking or goofing around. Just riding the waves. Then everyone would come in and give thanks to God for the day."

I stood there smiling at this image of surfing with Jesus. I looked at him, taking in his excitement at this idea. "That's a great image, Sam. I think you're right that Jesus wants to be where there's life. That's very cool." He smiled at me, pleased with himself. "Thank you for talking with me," I said. He could tell I meant it. "I'm going to think about that the next time I feel really alive—I'm going to think about Jesus being with me."

Three days after my encounter with Sam, I got an email from his mother. "For the first time in three years, Sam says he liked Sunday school. On the way home from church he told me he had a great conversation with you. He said he feels you're the only one who really understands him." The truth was that I didn't really understand Sam. I was just beginning to know him. But I did listen to him. I kept from trying to sell him my own agenda. I allowed him to be himself. I delighted in his ideas and vision. I tried to just be present to him and give him a listening ear to explore his reflections on Jesus. I believe that Sam was really telling his mom that he enjoyed being heard. That he liked being able to express his ideas, and that in expression he discovered a new sense of himself and God.

Because of this interaction I began to engage Sam about the meaning of worship, about Jesus and his message of love. As I allowed Sam to express his ideas and experience of God, he was willing to listen to my thoughts, to Scripture, and to tradition. We were in dialogue, searching side-by-side, wondering along with the first disciples, "Who then is this, that even the wind and the sea obey him?" (Mark 4:41).

## 2. Let me tell you a story.

Christians are people who tell stories. We tell stories of slavery and exodus, of faithfulness and pride, of sacrifice and betrayal. For Christians the sacred stories found in the Bible are part of the great story of God, through Jesus, reconciling the world. But we do more than just tell these stories; we believe and live into these stories. We allow them to penetrate our understanding of life, to form and shape us, to guide and articulate our own experience. The stories of Scripture are windows into the nature of God and humanity and our relationship to one another. They are stories that help us repent, heal, learn, grow and stretch toward God's love and wholeness. Christians believe Scripture locates us. It helps us name our experience and points us to deeper ways in which we can experience God's love and compassion for humanity.

Every time I lead a class or program with young people, I try to tell a story from the Bible. I want the young people in my life to marinate in the stories of Scripture, not only so they'll know that Jesus had 12 disciples and Moses was raised in Egypt, but also so they can see how God is with us. I want them to hear the stories of the Bible until

naming

the Bible begins to read them—until they can interpret their situation through the images, situations, and stories of the Bible.

For eight years I led week-long retreats entitled "Sabbath" for youth ministers. Each retreat I would choose an account from Scripture in which someone encountered Jesus. This story would become the foundational passage for the week. Each day we would read a verse or two from the chosen passage during morning and evening prayer. We would lead prayer exercises on the story, and each morning one of the leaders would offer a simple meditation on the days' passage. By the end of the retreat, participants had heard the same story of an encounter with Jesus numerous times. They had prayed with it, studied it, worshipped with it, and meditated on it.

I often noticed a change in people's experience of the story over the course of the week. For example, if we focused on the passage from Mark 1:40-45 in which Jesus heals a leper, I'd watch as people first encountered the story as a lesson: *Jesus is a healer. Those in need of healing should turn to Jesus.* As the week went on and they prayed with it over and over, their experience of the story became more rich and textured. People began to find themselves in the passage. They could feel themselves as the leper, bringing their sorrow and pain to Jesus. Or they found themselves as townspeople listening to the leper's story of healing, feeling jealous that they weren't the one touched by Jesus. Other times participants found themselves in the countryside with Jesus, avoiding the crowds or feeling compassion with Jesus as the leper pleaded for help. The way in which we continually sought to enter the story of Scripture helped people locate themselves in their lives with God and then pointed them toward new ways in which they could grow in relationship with Jesus.

We try to create the same atmosphere with young people. We don't just want them to read or hear the stories of Jesus; we want to allow them to enter into those stories. We give them invitations to find themselves in Scripture, to use the words and images of the

Bible to deepen their experience of God. We ask them to tell us their feelings as the leper approaches Jesus. We invite them to place themselves imaginatively in the passage and tell us what they see. We ask them to tell us where they've seen or experienced the story in Scripture taking place today. These and other exercises help young people develop a vocabulary of faith—a way of navigating their lives with God, placing them in conversation with Christians who have traveled the journey for 2,000 years. As youth become familiar with the stories of faith, as they begin to see those stories illuminating their own life experiences, theological conversation comes naturally, grounded in what they've felt and known through the testimony of the biblical writers.

### 3. Testimony.

Not only is it important for young people to hear the stories of Scripture, it's also important for them to hear the stories of other Christians who follow Jesus. I remember leading a series of youth classes in which I'd invited different members of the congregation to meet with the youth and tell them about their own relationships with God throughout their lives. I brought in a retired sailor, a middle-aged real estate saleswoman, a young stockbroker, and a woman who ran a funeral home. All of them talked about their encounters with God and explained why they called themselves followers of Jesus. The youth were riveted to hear stories of great doubt, debilitating tragedy, unanswered prayer, and mystical experiences of Jesus' companionship. At the end of each testimony, I allowed kids to ask questions. It was easy to see that most of the youth's questions dealt with their own struggles: "Did you ever fall in love with someone who wasn't a Christian?" "How could you keep following God after your mother died?" "Did you ever do drugs when you were young?"

Youth not only want adults who will listen, but also yearn for adults who will engage them in truthful conversation. I find young people eager to hear the struggles and interior lives of adults. They

naming

want to hear the experiences of adult Christians who have struggled to make sense of tragedy, sin, and temptation. They want to know how adults discern how to act in a secular world obsessed with sex, greed, and violence. These testimonies and dialogues help give words and expression to the burgeoning struggles and experiences that exist in the lives of youth. It gives them a perspective from which to make sense of their own yearnings and disappointments.

One time I helped organize a meeting in which the young men in our youth group met with the adult men of the church, while the young women in our group met with the adult women of our church. At each gathering the teenagers were invited to ask any question they wanted about what it was like to be an adult Christian. I facilitated the meeting between the younger and older men. After a few minutes of awkwardness, one of the young men asked, "How did you know what God wanted you to do with your life?" After some silence one man said he initially thought he'd be a grocer like his father, but then he decided to go to college. He studied engineering and became a civil engineer, but after a few years felt unsatisfied. So when a friend invited him to help start a software company, he quit his job. Other men told similar stories of transition, giving no clear picture as to how God had led each of them into his particular career.

A second student then asked what the men had learned about relating to women. There was an even longer pause. One man said he felt like he understood his wife when they first got married, but then discovered he didn't know her at all. Even now, as a man in his 50s, he felt as though he was still learning how to relate to her. Other men talked about divorce, broken relationships, and how difficult it was to know how to relate to another person.

A third young person asked how the men decided to commit to the Christian faith. Again we heard mixed stories of heartfelt commitments to Jesus followed by years of doubt and abandoning the faith. Some spoke of still feeling like they had one foot in the church and one foot out the door. As our time drew to a close, I asked the youth to express what they'd gathered from listening to the men. One boy looked thoughtful for a while and then said to the men, "You guys don't have anything figured out, do you?" We all broke out in laughter. Then the same young man said, "That's actually quite a relief. I feel so confused at times, and it seems so hard to know how God wants me to live. I've never told anyone that before. I always feel like I'm supposed to act confident—like I know what I'm doing and where I'm headed. It's such a relief to know I can be a Christian and not have everything figured out." Hearing adults talk about the ambiguity and struggle of living the life of faith helped articulate the experience of many young people in that church and opened up further conversation between the generations in that community.

Creating settings where youth can hear the testimonies of other Christians, as well as express their own, helps them broaden and claim their experiences of God in new ways. Not only is it helpful for youth to hear the testimonies of adult Christians, but it's also extremely powerful for them to hear the stories and testimonies of those Christians we call saints. I often tell young people the story of St. Francis and his struggle with his father. I tell them of St. Anthony and his sojourn to the desert after the death of his parents. I tell them about modern saints like Howard Thurman and his life of prayer and racial integration. All of this becomes both a comfort and an inspiration as their own experiences of faith are illumined and broadened through hearing the experiences of other lovers of God.

## 4. Beyond Words.

Of course, words aren't always needed to help youth name their experiences of God. Some of the most powerful expressions of faith in the Bible are actions or symbols with few words attached: the woman who bathes and anoints Jesus' feet, the hemorrhaging woman who touches Jesus' cloak, the poor widow who places two coins in the offering, the crowd waving palm branches as Jesus enters the holy

naming

city. These symbolic acts contain more than words can express and are, in many ways, more powerful than simple verbal expressions of faith. Youth often struggle to find words to express their deepest feelings. That's why it can be very helpful, from time to time, to invite them to name their experiences of God in ways that don't rely on words.

In chapter 11, I gave examples of prayer exercises that involve colors and artistic expression. I've found the use of these and other art media can help youth explore and express their relationships with God in symbolic language. That's especially important for churched kids, who often develop habits of expression and Christian understanding that insulate them from engaging God in new ways. I like to hang the artwork and prayer images created by youth in the places where I meet with them. This not only honors their expression, but also begins to testify to the diverse relationships people have with God.

Inviting youth to find objects in nature to express their lives in God can also be revelatory. Once after leading kids in a silent prayer exercise, I invited them to walk around the church grounds and find an object that best expressed their relationship with God. After 20 minutes or so, the youth returned. I encouraged volunteers to share their objects with the group. One boy, who was quite shy and rarely spoke up, raised his hand and said, "I found something that exactly expresses my relationship with God." He then asked us all to gather around him. In his palm was a small purple flower bud. He held it out for all of us to see. He carefully closed his hand for a moment or two. When he uncurled his fingers, the flower, responding to the warmth of his hand, was opening. We all looked on in wonder as he smiled, pleased by this simple expression of his life in God.

For years my wife and I have designed interactive prayer spaces that allow young people and youth ministers to engage their relationship with God through a variety of symbols. We've designed prayer spaces according to particular lessons or conference themes that allow youth to pray in new ways. For example, one conference focused on the different images of Jesus in the Gospel of John—images of light, bread, living water, the vine. We found a room that seemed quiet and comfortable. The room was low-lit with candles. In one corner we placed a planted vine with many branches. On a small placard we invited kids to pray about the parts of their lives in which Jesus seemed absent—places where they wanted Jesus to "abide" with them. The youth were then invited to tie a ribbon on the vine branches as a symbol of their desire to stay close to Jesus.

Another corner was draped in thick black fabric. One red candle stood burning atop a small table surrounded by sand. "I am the light of the world," was written at the base of the candle. Again, a small placard invited youth to pray about the dark places in their own lives and in the world. Kids were then encouraged to take a candle from the basket, light it, and place it in the sand next to the Christ candle. Another corner of the prayer room had a small pool of flowing water with lush plants growing at the water's edge. Pitchers of water were placed near the pool and people were invited to pray by the water's edge, reflecting on the ways in which God was seeking to pour living water into their lives and the life of the world. Seekers were then invited to pour a glass of cool water and drink it as a symbol of their desire to receive the life Jesus offers.

These kinds of creative, symbolic rituals and acts can help youth find new ways of uncovering and expressing their lives in God. Over time, rituals might emerge that become important to a particular group of kids. One church I worked with has a "prayer net"—a large fishing net hung on one side of the youth room. At the end of each gathering, the youth share their prayer concerns with one another and pray. After each prayer concern is spoken, one of the kids ties a colored ribbon on the net as a symbol of that prayer. When a prayer concern is too personal or painful for a young person to share, he

naming

or she can simply tie one of the ribbons to the net without saying a word. After a year the net was covered in ribbons—even though the group has no more than 18 kids. What does it mean for these kids to enter the youth room week after week and see this prayer net, slung heavy with prayers? What does it mean for young people to have the opportunity to express the prayers of their hearts without speaking a word? Maybe in this ritual they will come closer to the Holy Spirit who prays within us "with sighs too deep for words."

## Faith Takes Time

Helping youth find their way into the Christian tradition takes time. All kids—and especially those with little church background—need lots of time and patience before Christian words and language give meaning to their unique experiences of life and the Mystery we call God. When you develop a relationship with a young person, it's important to understand that you are beginning a conversation that will last many years, even a lifetime. It may be that for the whole first year of your relationship with a young man, for example, all you'll talk about is basketball. Every time you try to change the subject, he tolerates it—but as soon as he gets the chance, he turns the subject back to basketball. Then the second year all you'll talk about is girls. Despite interesting Bible studies, spiritual exercises, and inspiring worship services, you find that all he wants to discuss is the opposite sex. The third year you'll talk about his parents' divorce. Every conversation, no matter how informed and enlightened, will continually draw back to his relationship and troubles with his parents. The fourth year you'll find yourself discussing colleges and universities ad nauseam—entrance exams, grades, and SAT scores. Then a year later, after he's left your ministry and gone off to college, you'll be standing in line at a fast-food restaurant and notice this same young man who used to be in your church. You sit down together and out of the blue he looks up at you and says, "Do you ever wonder what life's about?"

For five years you've been talking about basketball, dating, divorce, parents, and college. You've been waiting for five years to talk about the meaning of life. You've been waiting to talk about the Christian faith. Now, suddenly, because you were patient, because you were present, he's ready to talk to you about matters of the heart. Now he wants to listen to your understanding of life with God. Now he wants to find words that speak to his experience. He trusts you because he's known your patient companionship. After five years he trusts you enough to ask, "What's all this Christianity stuff about anyway...and why do you go to this church?" And that's when it's time to talk. That's the time for words.

nurturing

13

Before integrating contemplation, I did youth ministry very, very differently. We didn't eat dinner together. I planned the program to a T. I never ventured from the plan. I made it go, no matter who got anxious. (More often it was me.) Any distraction from the kids only made things worse as I plowed through the program. The youth ministry wasn't so open to intimacy, which comes from listening. I hardly noticed what was going on with the kids or advisors. I was often too busy with the agenda to even notice God's presence and rarely felt grateful in the ministry.

I'm slower now, and more intentional about what I do, although more often than not the intention is spontaneous. The intention is focused on one another and on God. I ask more questions—better questions—of God, of myself, of the kids. I go off on more tangents, which often lands us in a better place (paying better attention to that still small voice). I look for Belovedness. I might not be doing youth ministry any more, but I trust that God will work (in me, through me, and in spite of me, if necessary).

—JEN BUTLER, ASSOCIATE PASTOR, WESTMINSTER PRESBYTERIAN CHURCH, EUGENE, OREGON

Live your life as a work of art.

—ABRAHAM HESCHEL (ADDRESSING THE YOUTH OF NORTH AMERICA)

Through prayer and presence we're better able to help kids notice and name their lives in God. Our next venture is to help each young person nurture this growing relationship of love.

It's naive to believe our ministries can simply be times of sitting and listening to youth. Young people like to do stuff—and so do adults. The immediate question that most youth ministers, churches, and parents face every week is "What are we going to do with the kids?" There are Sunday school classes, confirmation programs, youth group meetings, and outings to plan. We can seek to be open and present to youth within these activities, but how do we create youth ministry programs that aren't in direct contrast to the contemplative spirit we seek to foster? Once we begin to help kids notice and name their relationship with God, how do we create a ministry program that nurtures and deepens that relationship?

# Follow the Thread

Up in the wine country north of San Francisco, there lives an Orthodox priest who's spent the past 30 years of his life in prayer and solitude. A friend of mine spent a week with him in his hermitage. Except for morning and evening prayer, the two of them kept silence for seven days. At the end of the week, my friend, who is also Orthodox, asked the priest for a word—some offering of wisdom to help him on his journey of faith. The reclusive priest gave him three: "Follow the thread."

Many times I've wished God would wrap a rope around my waist and pull me where I need to go. Following Jesus is often a murky endeavor, clouded with doubt and second-guessing. Ministry is no different. I often question whether the relationships, teaching, and programs I'm offering young people are responding to the needs of the youth and the movement of the Holy Spirit. I want clear signs and signals from God (as well as from the youth!) regarding how to act

nurturing

and lead. Yet God continues to speak in a still, small voice. My experience is much closer to the guiding words of the praying priest. There seems to be a thin thread that runs through the noise and activity of my life and ministry. It's a thread I lose track of at times; a thread that requires me to slow down, look, and feel in order not to lose it; a thread that, though thin and fragile, leads to life.

In ministry we seek to follow the thread. We seek to notice the ways in which God is moving in the ministry. We pay attention to when kids become responsive and alive. We notice where the needs and hurts of young people are coming to the surface. We listen and talk and discern these experiences of God, and then we respond. Our programs and activities always seek to grow out of the needs of youth and the movement of the Holy Spirit. This takes prayer, discernment, patience, and creativity.

Sadly, most churches (and ministers) are so busy trying to imitate other larger, "successful" churches that they don't take the time to notice how God is uniquely present within their own congregations and youth. There is a lack of trust in their own gifts, prayer life, and capacities to create an effective youth ministry.

The word *minister* comes from words meaning to "attend" or "serve". The ministries we develop, the teachings we offer, and the activities we do with youth all must come out of "attending" to the needs of kids and the guidance of the Holy Spirit. This is what it means to "follow the thread" in ministry. We notice the little places where life meets life—where God is breaking into the lives of our young people. We then create programs and curriculums that follow the life that arises in the ministry.

Let me illustrate further. Below are three examples of ministries that nurture life in God because they respond to noticing the "thread" of God's Spirit.

contemplative youth ministry

## The Bread of Life

A friend of mine is married to a part-time pastor of a mid-sized church outside of Anchorage, Alaska. After much prodding by a committee of eager parents, she and her husband agreed to start a youth ministry at their church. They began with the traditional youth programs—a teen Sunday school class and a mid-week youth group meeting. Parents, excited to have something for their teenagers, immediately sent their teens to each of the programs. Unfortunately, many of the youth had been dragged to Sunday morning worship throughout their childhood and had developed a resistance to anything church-related. During Sunday morning classes, kids sat slouched and sleepy-eyed, their communication skills reduced to grunts and nods. At youth group meetings they disrupted any attempt to talk, study, or practice anything connected to the Christian faith. Claiming it was "too much like school," the youth informed the two youth leaders that they wanted youth group to be a social time to visit friends without "all the boring stuff about God."

Each week Winnie and her husband gathered people together to pray, listen, discern, and respond to what they were noticing in the youth group. One week it became clear that they needed to interact with young people outside of the formal youth group setting. Winnie began to seek out kids intentionally during potlucks and after worship when the youth hung out at the coffee table. One Sunday after worship she sat with two 13-year-old girls and began to talk about how they spend their Saturdays. Winnie mentioned that she liked to bake cookies. The two girls lit up, replying that they too loved to bake, but didn't get much time to do it. Winnie asked if the girls would bring their favorite recipes and ingredients to church the following Sunday, and after worship they would bake in the church kitchen. The girls were ecstatic.

The following week the two girls came to church carrying cooking supplies and baking ingredients, accompanied by a number of friends. After worship they all spent the whole afternoon creating different cookie concoctions and talked openly about their lives at school and at home. Winnie was so taken by the girls' openness and enthusiasm around baking that she asked if they would be willing to come to church early the following Sunday and bake bread for communion. Again, the girls were excited by the idea—they'd never baked bread before—and agreed to come. The following Sunday the girls arrived just as the sun was coming up. They gathered in the church kitchen and began making the bread dough. They asked Winnie questions about communion—where it began and why Christians practice it. They asked Winnie about her marriage to a minister and her relationship to the church. Winnie later told me this was one of the most significant discussions she'd had with young people at that church. They agreed to meet again to bake bread for the service.

Two years later Winnie continues to meet with a group of girls to bake bread for communion. They often bake more than enough for the service and take the extra loaves to a local food shelter. When I called Winnie to ask her how it was going, she told me, "The kids really see this as a service they offer the church and a way that they're living out their faith. On Sundays when I'm absent, they still show up and faithfully bake the bread. Last Sunday one of the church elders came into the kitchen and watched. He noticed that the kids were so absorbed in their baking that for several minutes no one spoke a word. They just quietly worked, kneading and shaping the bread. The morning bread-baking has become a significant part of their life with God."

What's significant in this experience is that Winnie did not engage the kids in baking because of a book or program. She wasn't trying to create a "Baking Model of Ministry." She simply began to pay attention to the youth, to listen to them, to notice where they came alive—and then followed that thread. In following that thread of life she discovered a way of ministering with those young girls that drew upon her own gifts and interests, a ministry "program" in which the youth felt free to explore their faith.

## I Was Sick and You Took Care of Me

Another friend of mine ministers with youth in an inner-city Episcopal church in Richmond, Virginia. The church holds an annual "Community Action Fair," where various nonprofit agencies that serve downtown Richmond set up booths at the church and share information about their programs. Every year my friend Steve asks the youth to learn about the different organizations and then choose one to volunteer in for one day as part of their confirmation class. One year a representative of the children's ward of the Medical College of Virginia set up an information booth. A group of teens visited the booth and spoke with the volunteer from the Medical College. The children's ward was located just a block from the church, and the teens were surprised to learn that many of the children there were suffering from terminal illnesses.

The next week Steve gathered the youth and asked them to report which organization they'd chosen to volunteer with. The young people who'd met the representative from the Medical College spoke first. They told the rest of the group about the work of the children's ward, about the dying children, and about the college's need for volunteers to spend time caring for the children. These youth then proposed that the whole group serve at the ward—and that they not do it for a single day, but commit to doing it one Sunday a month for the next year.

For the next hour the youth and ministry team discussed the proposal. Finally, they agreed that they would volunteer together on a Sunday afternoon and see what it was like before making a year-long commitment. After the meeting the youth ministry leaders gathered for prayer and discernment. They were feeling pessimistic about committing the youth group to spend one Sunday a month at the children's ward. Wouldn't it disrupt their teaching curriculum? Would

nurturing

parents be upset that their kids weren't in Sunday school? Would kids grow tired of volunteering? Volunteering at the hospital was a good deed, but was it really the mission of the youth ministry program to be providing regular volunteers for the hospital?

For the next two weeks the youth ministry leaders sent out information about the volunteer day at the children's ward. When the day came to visit the ward, the youth program had its highest turnout of the year. The teens arrived early to make cards and banners, plan games, and collect storybooks. They walked to the ward en masse and, after a brief orientation with the hospital staff, spread out among the children's wing to sing songs, deliver cards, play games, and befriend the sick children.

Afterward, the youth gathered back at the church. They shared their experiences and then spent a long time praying about the children they'd seen. After the kids left, the leaders met again. They prayed and listened and tried to discern how the Holy Spirit was seeking to guide the ministry. It was clear there was a deep, authentic sense of excitement from the kids about serving at the hospital. They reflected on Jesus' words, "When I was sick, you cared for me." Then one parent serving on the ministry team shared that a classmate of many of our kids who had died of cancer when they were in grade school. She recalled the impact the death of this young child had made on the whole school. She added that her own son still referred to it, even though many years had passed. "I think these kids have a heart for dying children," she reflected. "I think these youth are called to serve these children, and we need to respond."

The leaders decided to shift their curriculum (an expensive and popular one they had recently purchased). They would drop a lesson plan each month and replace it with a visit to the children's ward. They would help the youth design and plan a program for the dying children. They would start a new teaching session on the Christian perspective of death and grief. They would contact the local hospice and train the youth in the necessary skills for spending time with dying children.

Three years later the Sunday morning youth program at St. Paul's Episcopal Church is still grounded in monthly visits to the nearby children's ward of the Medical College of Virginia. This ministry wasn't garnered from a book or program. It came from a praying youth ministry community that was attentive to the youth and willing to respond to the nudging of the Holy Spirit. It was difficult, at first, to alter their plans and teaching design. But because the leaders were attentive, they knew their real task was to follow Jesus' lead—so they built a ministry around connecting the young people to the children in the hospital.

## Bowling for Jesus

I spent three years working with a Lutheran church set back in the Cascade Mountains of Eastern Washington. It's a small but vibrant congregation with a commitment to social justice. In developing its youth ministry program, the church had attracted a group of adults committed to contemplative prayer. They were interested in developing a contemplative approach to youth ministry and attended various training events that I co-led presenting many of the ideas and principles in this book. The church formed a small covenant community of adults who prayed together and followed the "liturgy for discernment" as they led the youth ministry. The adults had been deeply nurtured by contemplative prayer and wanted to share it with the youth. They began to implement dramatic changes in the youth program. They designed the youth room to be more of a prayer space with a small altar and candles. Teaching times became focused on exploring various traditional forms of contemplative prayer. Games were replaced by long periods of silence and journaling. The adults were ecstatic at the new program they'd created and enjoyed the times of prayer and quiet with the youth. There was only one problem: The kids hated it.

nurturing

Week after week as the youth leaders became more focused on teaching contemplative prayer, the kids became agitated and bored, and sometimes they even fell asleep during long prayer periods. Some of the youth, frustrated with the silence, just stopped showing up to church. The adults, on the other hand, stayed committed to engaging kids in contemplative prayer. Many of them had undergone life-transforming experiences in prayer and deeply hoped the youth would have similar experiences. The tension came to a climax when the adults decided to make the annual summer mission trip a contemplative retreat in a New Mexico desert. The trip would be a Christian "vision quest," much like Jesus' time in the wilderness before he began his public ministry. The kids would spend most of the week in solitude, silence, and prayer.

The youth revolted; no one wanted to go on the trip. The leaders were surprised by the resistance and confused as to how to respond. Should they insist they knew what was best for the teenagers and continue with the spiritual retreat? The following weeks were filled with uncertainty. The adult leaders continued to meet for contemplative prayer and discernment. They tried to deepen their attention to the youth, seeking to notice the moments when the kids were most alive. They talked, listened, prayed, and sought to discern God's leading. As they shared they began to notice their own attachments and projections within the youth ministry. They explored the painful prospect of abandoning their plans for a contemplative retreat in New Mexico. Some adults were grieved by the idea of giving up the retreat. As they deepened their reflection, one woman bravely admitted that much of her energy regarding the retreat came out of her own desire to attend such an event. She recognized that she wanted to lead a contemplative retreat in part because she wished that someone had taken her on a contemplative retreat when she was a teenager. Another woman realized she felt deeply called to a contemplative life, and the contemplative retreat was the primary reason she wanted to serve in the youth ministry. Without it, she wasn't sure she was called to work with kids. Yet another volunteer talked about his impulse to finish what he'd started. He noticed how frustrated he felt about leting go of an event he'd already spent many hours working on.

As the group continued to pray and take "a long loving look at the real," they were forced to admit the retreat was more about them than the kids. When they told the youth the retreat was cancelled, the announcement was received with whoops and cheers. The adults noticed they soon felt relieved as well. But now they were faced with a programmatic hole. How would they organize the youth program now that they had abandoned their contemplative curriculum? The volunteer leaders decided to let go of their previous agenda and simply look for signs of life and energy among the youth. To their dismay they recognized one primary place where the kids seemed to be most alive: the bowling alley. Every time they took the youth bowling, the kids seemed to light up. The adults noticed that the divisions between social groups quickly fell away as kids slapped each other high fives, cheered on teammates, and sipped soda at the score table. Even the adults got into the act, laughing right along with the kids. At their next discernment meeting, everyone in the leadership group had to admit that the youth group seemed closer to living into the kingdom of God at the bowling alley than in a silent prayer exercise. They began to explore how they could make bowling a regular part of the group. The next week they told the youth they would go bowling once a month—with one twist. The group would have dinner together at the church beforehand and then walk to the alley together. The leaders felt dinner and the walk would provide greater opportunities for conversation and relationships with the kids.

At first the leaders felt guilty about offering a youth program that seemed like nothing more than a night of fun and games. But over time, they discovered deeper issues that had previously gone unattended. There were new kids in the group who felt alienated; there were tensions between more privileged and less privileged kids.

Through bowling and play, the leaders began to realize that God had a deeper agenda. God wanted the kids to become a community, to cross social and economic lines, to learn to pray and care for one another despite their differences.

Frank Rogers, professor of Christian Education at Claremont School of Theology, served as one of the scholars involved in the Youth Ministry and Spirituality Project. After three years of observing the youth ministry in this congregation, he offered this summary of this Lutheran church's attempt to nurture faith in its young people:

> This church experimented with a contemplative approach to youth ministry. In doing so, they felt like total failures. The teens resisted the spiritual practices of prayer and retreat, and the adults, mired in frustration, scrapped the best contemplative curriculum they'd been able to find. But a contemplative approach to youth ministry does not entail teaching youth to become contemplatives. It entails a leadership committed to a contemplative process of its own that enables them to see ways of crafting programmatic action that authentically participates with God in nurturing life and faith in young people...Where other leaders, enamored by their own creativity but blind to the cries of their youth, may have pushed their own agenda, these youth leaders let go of their own designs, listened deeply for the movements of God, and crafted actions that followed the pulse of their discernment. As such, they have much to teach us about the nature of authentic ministry.

# Contemplative Karaoke

It was just past 10 p.m. on the fifth night of a Youth Ministry and Spirituality Project retreat for youth and youth ministers on the campus of San Francisco Theological Seminary. Seventeen-year-old John Schwehn was going through a full-blown voice-change as he belted out the lyrics to the 1970s disco hit "I Will Survive." Ninety teenagers and adults sat whooping and clapping to the disco beat as John crowed to the karaoke machine and jigged something I'd call, "The Wounded-Chicken Two-Step." It was then, in the middle of this funky, ridiculous, joyful vamp, that I looked toward the back of the room and saw something familiar—something that caused me to cringe and look for cover. It was the face that appears regularly in my ministry with young people. This face can possess a variety of persons in vastly different settings, yet consistently evokes the same feelings of shame and punishment. It's the "You're in BIG trouble" face—and it has followed me throughout my ministry.

On this particular night the face was found on two middle-aged seminary students who stood at the back of the room, their bodies rigidly defying the karaoke disco around them, as if to say, "We will not boogie. We will not get down!" These two women met my eyes and gestured stiffly that I was to follow them outside. A few steps from the music they began to bear down, "Do you know what time it is? Do you understand that some of us have classes in the morning? Don't you know it's eight minutes past the 10 p.m. sound ordinance?" They looked at me like I was a drug trafficker. I smiled sheepishly, apologized, and promised to stop the karaoke. Satisfied but still disgruntled, they asked me, "So what are all these kids doing here on campus anyway?" I perked up, eager to change the tone of our conversation, and explained excitedly that this was a retreat for youth and youth leaders from across the country who were together exploring a "contemplative approach" to youth ministry.

nurturing

Their faces scrunched up like I'd poured spoiled cream in their coffee. "Did you say 'contemplative'?" one of them asked me incredulously.

"Yes," I said, confused by her reaction.

"That" she said, pointing to the room where two kids holding stuffed animals were now doing a night-club medley of Veggie Tales songs, "is not contemplative!"

It's surprising to many, including the two seminary students on our campus, to find a ministry that claims to promote contemplative awareness leading a retreat that includes karaoke, body-surfing, ultimate Frisbee, and a game called "Pony" in which kids and adults dance and sing, "Here we go, gonna ride my pony, riding around on my big fat pony." (The night after karaoke we were busted again by local residents and seminary students for playing Pony after 10 p.m.) What happened to silence? Where's the mystical prayer? What about journaling or solitude, Taizé music and *lectio divina*?

North American Christianity is a religion of dichotomies: you're either into spirituality or social justice, contemporary or traditional worship, educational or entertaining youth programs, "being" or "doing." Many in the church, stuck in this either-or thinking, perceive that contemplative youth ministry is focused solely on prayer, silence, and solitude. We associate contemplation with monk robes, candles, and sitting Buddhas. Like the seminary students I encountered, we find it difficult to imagine a "spiritual" retreat (much less a "contemplative" retreat) engaging kids in playful (and sometimes just plain goofy) activities.

The purpose of integrating contemplative presence in youth ministry is not to turn kids into monks, nor is it to make us experts in contemplative prayer; it is to deepen our awareness of God, others, and self so that we might become fully alive. Jesus promises, "I have come that you might have life." Our task as ministers is to give young

contemplative youth ministry

people the space, relationships, experiences, and knowledge needed to hold that Life.

Engaging kids solely in contemplative exercises is unnatural, because contemplative prayer does not lead to more contemplative prayer—it leads to authentic action. Activities in the youth ministry are no longer chosen frantically from resource books; instead the youth ministry becomes more responsive to the needs of the youth and the movement of the Holy Spirit. We begin to hold our programs lightly, realizing they can be changed or discarded if they impede God's desire for love. We trust God more, knowing the Holy Spirit will be faithful in—and maybe even in spite of—our programs. We give ourselves a break and have more compassion for lesson plans that fall flat and outings that don't live up to our hopes and expectations. Through greater prayer and presence, we notice the moments of connection between youth and God and try and build our programs accordingly. Then, little by little, usually beneath our own awareness, the youth ministry begins to become alive with the Spirit of God. Increasingly there is real play filled with a sense of celebration and fun, rather than competitiveness and hyperactive excitement. Discussions become engaging rather than alienating and prescriptive. Mission trips and social justice activities begin to spring from compassion instead of guilt. Even prayer experiences grow hospitable and ordinary, less pristine and "otherworldly." The ministry becomes something unique and natural to our community, rather than a cookie-cutter "franchise" ministry imported from a mega-church.

As our interactions with youth become infused with prayer and relationship, as our ministries become more attentive to the movement of God, as we become more intentional about helping kids notice the way Jesus seeks to befriend them, our programs and actions will become more natural and responsive to the real needs of kids—and more receptive to the deep desire of God that moves within us.

nurturing

What *does* a contemplative approach to youth ministry look like? It looks like youth engaged in centering prayer as well as body surfing. It looks like kids doing *lectio divina* as well as critical study of the Bible. It looks like solitude as well as service projects, contemplative worship as well as disco karaoke. As Jesus points out again and again, it's not the method but the spirit—the love and awareness behind our activities—that make them Christian.

# beyond fear

# 14

For me the key was learning to listen to God. Through the silence, spiritual direction, and a focus on contemplative listening to others, I began to listen in a totally different way. I began to listen for God in others, listen between the words, actions, and experiences with others to hear how God was present. I began to realize I must center myself in God so I can be present to God in all that I do. I began to understand that only when I was centered in him was I able to turn outward to others. In fact, it was only as I centered myself in God that I began to reach out to others. This not only affected my work in youth ministry, but probably had the greatest impact on how I related to my own family, my own teenagers at home.

—BOB EISELT, ACCOUNTANT, VOLUNTEER YOUTH LEADER, BETHLEHEM LUTHERAN CHURCH, BAYPORT, MINNESOTA

Adults have to show kids that they're loved by God. They can tell you as much as they want, but they have to show you in some way. They have to show you that no matter what you do, even if you drop lasagna on the couch, it'll be okay—like, "We'll get over it. The couch was ugly in the first place. One more stain won't kill it. Life goes on." This is so much easier than if they just keep telling you like, "Hey, you're the beloved of God. Just believe it." It's easier when they show it to you and you can do stupid stuff, and you can tell that they love you, no matter what

—AMANDA FREY, AGE 15, HOUSTON, TEXAS

I'm in a downtown church doing a youth ministry consultation. So far I've only met with the adult power brokers—elders, staff, and parents. It's late on a Saturday afternoon, but I've asked the pastor if I could spend some time with the youth. Using a variety of tactics—pizza, threats, and manipulation—the youth director is able to round up 30 kids. I tell kids the situation: "I'm a youth ministry 'expert' flown in from San Francisco. The parents and members of this church want to help you make this faith and this church your own. They don't know what to do. They want me to make recommendations. What do you want me to say to them?"

There's silence as the group measures my words against my appearance. There are some awkward glances at peers. Then a young girl about 13 years old blurts out, "Don't be afraid of us." Other kids nod their heads. "Tell them to stop being afraid of us. We're their kids."

As I spoke further with these kids, I began to get a greater sense of what they wanted to say to the adults. They were trying to say: "Don't hold us at arm's length. Don't keep us distant. Don't pawn us off to a program, curriculum, or outside expert. After all, we're your children. We eat with you at your table. We listen in on your conversations. We sleep in the rooms next to yours. We're not an outside group. We come from your bodies. We're as close as the deepest hope within you—as close as your very hearts. Don't be afraid of us. Yes, we get frustrated when we don't understand your words or actions, and when you don't understand ours. Yes, we have energy and like to move, talk, and play. Yes, we are irritating and contrary at times—but we're trying to find our way in the world. We're trying to test reality, find its limits—see what ground is sandy and what ground is solid enough to stand on. We're really no different from you. Don't be afraid of us. We don't know who we are. But meanwhile we need someone to accept and accompany us. We need love and companionship. Because, although our bodies are different, at the level of the heart, we're really a lot like you."

Don't be afraid of us. What does it mean? It means staying close to our young people. It means being vulnerable and open to them. It means staying close to our own hearts, the temples where God's Spirit dwells. It means ending our search for an outside fix, a mediator between youth and us. It means churches facing their children on their own, with nothing but their own desire for relationship and their own testimony and practice of life. It means the solution to the "youth ministry question" can only be found with and among young people. It means trusting that the Mystery of God that works within each of us will give birth to new openings to life and relationship.

Four years ago the leaders of First United Methodist Church in Valparaiso, Indiana, were faced with a crisis involving skateboarders. It seemed the sidewalks, paved parking lot, and cement steps of the church had become a popular gathering place for local teen skaters. Every day kids in baggy clothes and tilted baseball caps pushed their wheels across the church property, leaped and flipped their boards across the church sidewalks, and then spent the late afternoon grinding their "trucks" (the metal axle joints underneath their boards) against the cement steps. Soon the cement began to crumble and break. Upset by the damage to church property, the church leaders decided to replace the steps, install protective devices into the cement to prevent skating, and post signs outlawing loitering and skateboarding.

The youth director and the covenant community of adults who served the youth ministry went to the church leadership and asked them to reconsider their decision. For three years the group had met each week to pray and seek guidance on serving kids in the community. They asked if the leadership might see the presence of youth as a blessing and, instead of asking them to leave, find ways to develop and deepen relationships with them. After weeks of prayer and discernment, the church leaders decided to reverse their decision. They left the crumbling and scuffed cement steps and removed the signs outlawing skateboarders and loitering. The pastor told me, "We decided to let the church have the ugliest front steps in town."

The next day leaders of the church met with the teen skaters and informed them of the church's decision. They told the skateboarders they were welcome to skate on the church property and use the other church facilities as well. They gave the kids a tour of the church building and showed them where the bathrooms and kitchen were located. They took the youth into the church office and introduced them to the staff.

If you want to know what it means to share the presence of Jesus with young people, if you want to know more than I can tell you in this book, then drive an hour east of Chicago to Valparaiso, Indiana. Go spend an afternoon sitting on the curb across the street from the Methodist church. Then watch as kids come skating up to the steps, leaping and twirling, crashing their boards against the concrete in acrobatic feats of life and energy. Sit and watch as the church secretaries, the bookkeeper, the maintenance and pastoral staff walk up the crumbling steps. Watch as they stop to say hello. Watch as they converse with the scruffy street skaters. Watch as they take time from their work schedule to applaud as a boy shows off an especially difficult spin on his board. Sit and don't say a word. Just listen to the whir of the wheels on the pavement. Watch the young people running in and out of the church to get water and use the bathroom and then see. See if you don't find those crumbling steps beautiful.

# Appendix 1

The two charts in Appendix 1 are visual descriptions of contemplative youth ministry that were developed with the Youth Ministry and Spirituality Project.

Three Approaches to Youth Ministry is a simple comparison of the roles, theology, and objectives of contemplative youth ministry when compared to the "consumer" and "content" approaches to youth work. The "consumer" approach refers to those models of ministry that focus on entertaining youth, thereby reflecting the values and mores of the market culture. The "content" approach describes an educational model solely directed to the transfer of religious information. All of these descriptions are quite general; any youth ministry program will be a complex mixture of all of these approaches (and others). Yet the comparison helps to expose the intention of a contemplative approach to youth ministry in contrast to other forms of ministry.

The Contemplative Ministry Cycle charts the movements and tensions I've observed within a variety of congregations as they've engaged in contemplative youth ministry. Again, this cycle is a general description of the experience of contemplative youth ministry in a congregation. In real life it appears much more complex and messy. Yet, over time, these movements and tensions do become more and more clear within youth ministries that seek to integrate contemplative prayer and communal discernment.

appendix

# Three Approaches to Youth Ministry

| Consumer | Content | Contemplation |
|---|---|---|
| Anxiety / Fear | Complacency | Love |
| Faith is good fun. | Faith is conformity. Dogmatic literacy. | Faith is an ongoing relationship. |
| Program Director / Professional Christian | Instructor/Person with Answers | Spiritual Director— (points to the presence of God) theologically and biblically informed disciple |
| Chaperones | Classroom Aides | Seekers, Mentors, Elders |
| Civic Values | Religious Information/ Indoctrination | Way of Jesus / Christian Living |
| Passivity, entertainment, consumerism | Conformity, memorization, regurgitation | Action rooted in prayer and theological reflection |
| Religious Consumers | Potential Institutional Members | Spiritual Seekers, developing a way of life |
| Board Members / Status Quo | Religious Institutions | Body of Christ / The Living God |

contemplative youth ministry

# Contemplative Ministry Cycle

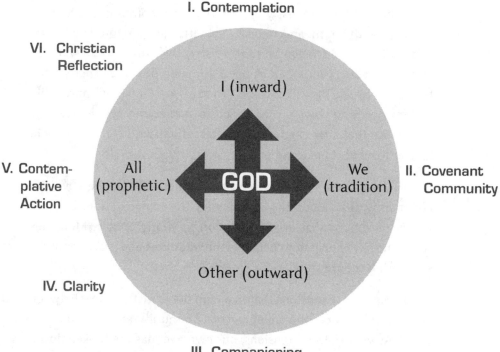

I. Contemplation

VI. Christian Reflection

I (inward)

V. Contemplative Action

All (prophetic)

GOD

We (tradition)

II. Covenant Community

Other (outward)

IV. Clarity

III. Companioning

I.  Contemplation. Sabbath and prayer help us pay attention to the presence of God in our life and the life of the ministry.

II.  Covenant Community. We join with others to tend the Spirit, deepen our discernment of God's call, and share the burdens of ministry.

III.  Companioning. We move out of prayer and community to accompany youth. Youth draw us out of prayer into service and care.

IV.  Clarity. As we pray and relate to youth, we begin to gain clarity as to how the Holy Spirit is calling us to act. This is the moment for discerning how (programs, relationships, activities?) we are called to minister with youth.

V.  Contemplative Action. Grounded in God and community, we begin to take action either on behalf of youth or with youth in service to a hurting world. Our programs and ministries are developed at this stage.

VI.  Christian Reflection. We reflect on our actions in light of Scripture and our Christian tradition. We identify how the Spirit is moving or blocked through our programs and actions.

I.  Contemplation. We start the cycle again. Returning to the Source—offering the ministry, ourselves, and our actions up to God. We begin again, waiting on God for guidance and renewal.

### The Inner Tensions:

As we live into this ministry cycle, our prayer, community life, relationships with youth, and ministry activities deepen, growing closer and closer to God's vision for the ministry. Over time, we may notice various tensions that break us open, bringing new life. There is the tension between the "I" and the "Thou"—my individual prayer life and my desire to move out of myself toward young people. We may also notice that as we increase our interactions with youth, we are in greater need of silence and prayer.

There is the tension between the ministry team, the covenant community that tends the tradition of the congregation, and the prophetic actions that arise in relation to young people. Ministries with youth will inevitably challenge the traditions and practices of the sponsoring congregation.

These are the tensions that make up the Christian life—between silence and service, the worshipping community and the suffering world. As we live these tensions, our own agendas are broken down. We become more aware and available to God's vision within our ministry, as well as in our individual and collective lives.

# Appendix 2

Below is a simple description of the movements of the liturgy for discernment. This handout is helpful when teaching the liturgy to volunteers.

## Liturgy for Discernment

### Ritual

(Silence, a song, lighting of a candle...some ritual that helps us recognize the presence of God.)

### Relating

(Checking-in. Attending to one another. "How are you?")

### Receiving

(Attending to God through prayer, either *Lectio Divina* or the Awareness Examen.)

### Ruminating

(Sharing with one another what we've noticed during the prayer.)

### Reflecting

(Touching on our call or mission. The group answers the following question: "Given what we've heard and shared, what is God's call to us?")

### Responding

(Out of listening, we do our work. We look at our business items.)

### Returning

(Closing prayer. Offering ourselves/efforts to God.)

# Appendix 3

## Retreat for Youth Ministry Volunteers

The following retreat outline was developed in the Youth Ministry and Spirituality Project. It is designed as a one-day gathering for youth ministry volunteers as they prepare to begin a year of ministry with youth.

### Purpose

This one-day retreat has the following objectives:

1. To begin building relationships among the ministry team.
2. To help individuals identify and deepen their call to this ministry.
3. To discover the collective identity and the unique vision that God is calling the group to undertake.
4. To help volunteers understand their roles and the way in which they will function as a group.
5. To begin to do some basic planning or organizing for the year.

### Setting

Choose a setting that will have limited distractions. Sometimes going to a retreat center or even spending a day at a different church allows a new openness and awareness among the group. Try not to hold this retreat at your church—it may be too distracting for staff and other members, and too tempting to make phone calls or fiddle with other tasks and projects during break times.

**Supplies**

Bible
Copy of "Liturgy for Discernment" for each person
Pens and paper for each person
Crayons and drawing paper or construction paper
Clay (optional)
Newsprint or whiteboard with pens
Candle
Matches
Tape recorder with contemplative/spiritual/reflective music
Snacks/drinks
Lunch (or plan for lunch out)


**Schedule**

| | |
|---|---|
| 8:00 a.m. | Retreat facilitator should arrive and set up room. |
| 9:00 | Volunteers should arrive. |
| 9-9:20 | Snacks, coffee, informal conversation. |
| 9:20 | **Begin Retreat.** Opening prayer or ritual to begin time together. |
| 9:25 | Facilitator should go over schedule and briefly outline the purpose of the retreat (see above). |
| 9:35 | **Ritual and Relating.** Check-in. Time for people to answer, "How are you today?" (This may take time if you have a large group...or you may want to break into smaller groups.) |
| 9:50 | ***Lectio Divina* (Receiving).** After everyone has shared, invite the group to a time of prayer. [You should already have a passage chosen for this exercise. Some good passages that focus on call and ministry include Isaiah 43:1-7; Jeremiah 1:4-8; Mark 4:1-9; Mark 10:13-16; Luke 4:16-21.] Explain how you are going to lead this prayer. For example, you might say, |

"In a moment I'll invite us to spend some time in God's presence. We'll have a couple minutes of silence then I'll read the Scripture passage three times. As I'm reading, listen for a word or phrase that seems to stand out, that seems addressed to you, like it's in bold. If a word comes to you, ignore the rest of the reading and just meditate on that word, repeating it over and over to yourself. See what images and insights come to you. After reflecting on the word, you may find yourself drawn to simply rest in the silence...enjoying God's presence, grateful for this time of prayer."

"We'll have about five minutes of silence after the second reading. [For people who have never done contemplative prayer, five minutes can be plenty of time. Add more time, however, if you sense the need for a longer period of quiet.] After five minutes I'll invite us to draw our attention back to the group and then I'll ask each of us to share what, if anything, has come to us during the prayer. Any questions? Then let us pray."

Lead the prayer, allowing for five minutes of silence. At the end of the five minutes, invite the group to offer thanks to God and then draw their attention back to the group.

10:05    **Ruminating.** Invite people to share the word that came to them and any insights or noticings that came out of the prayer. Remind people to speak as simply and succinctly as possible if the group is large.

10:20    **Reflecting.** Call. Ask the group, *"Given everything we've heard and shared, what is our call* (God's invitation to us) *this morning? What is God saying to us this morning as a group?"* The purpose of this question is for the group to begin to notice common images and insights from the sharing and begin to notice common ways that the group is being called to serve/live. Also be prepared that there may not be any connections.

| 10:30 | **Break** |
|---|---|
| 10:45 | **Prayer Exercise.** Invite the individuals in your group to engage in a prayer exercise with colors. Explain that this is not an art exercise but a time of prayer without words. You might say the following: |

*"The purpose of the prayer is to listen for the ways in which God is seeking to relate to you at this time in your life. We are listening for how God is calling each of us to live so that we might be clearer as to how this ministry is part of God's overall call in our lives. We'll do this through creating images of our individual lives. In a minute I'll invite you to a time of silent prayer. In this silence I want you to take a piece of paper and some colors, and then find a place by yourself somewhere in the room (or facility). Ask God to give you an image of your life at this time. It may contain images of different aspects of your life right now...it may be more impressionistic...just colors and designs. Don't try to force anything; just let the images or colors come as you pray* [You may want to use this time to explain your own understanding of call. Refer to some of the readings, notes from the in-service, or explain your own understanding or experience of call in order to give the group some ideas on what to pay attention to.]

| 11:15 | Have the group gather to share the images and reflections from the prayer. Ask them: |
|---|---|

1. *What do you notice about your relationship to God in this picture?*

2. *What seems to be God's invitation or call as you look at this image of your life?*

3. *How is this ministry part of your life as you look at this image?*

| 11:45 | At the end of the sharing period ask, *"Are there any common themes in our sharing?"* Spend some time discussing this question. |
|---|---|

appendix

| 12:30 | **Lunch** |
|---|---|
| 1:45 | **Covenant.** Create a covenant of how you hope to work together. Present some of the commitments in the original calling (hours each week, meeting times, etc.). Explain the roles of volunteers and the purpose of the ministry team. Create a "working covenant," a document that can be revised as the group engages in the ministry. |
| 3:00 | **Break** |
| 3:15 | **Liturgy for Discernment.** Hand out a description of the "Liturgy for Discernment" and go over the steps of the meeting. You might reflect on how many of these steps have been experienced and incorporated into the retreat this day. |
| 4:00 | **Business.** (Responding) Go over any agenda items—whatever tasks the group has for the ministry. |
| 5:00 | **Awareness Examen.** End with an Awareness Examen over the day. For what moment do people feel most grateful for this day? |
| 5:30 | **Returning.** Closing prayer. |
| 6:00 | **Dinner Together.** (It might be nice to invite family members of the ministry team to join in you in order to see the larger context in which this ministry operates.) |

# Appendix 4

## Guidelines for Leading a Prayer Exercise with Youth

The following comments and instructions evolved during my time in the Youth Ministry and Spirituality Project. Youth leaders in the project found these guidelines to be helpful reminders as they designed prayer experiences.

### HOSPITALITY

Before you begin, dedicate your efforts to God and trust that God will work through the exercise. Remind yourself that the prayer is not about you; it's about God.

Have a set order and time for the exercise. Have all materials ready and available. Think through how the exercise will take place. Create a welcoming space for prayer. Pay attention to the senses—is there beauty? Does the space help draw attention to God's presence?

### INVITATION

Describe the whole exercise to youth in simple terms. Make sure everyone understands how the exercise will proceed. Try to maintain an "experimental" tone during the invitation to prayer. Say something to the effect of "We're going to try an experiment in prayer. It may or may not be the way in which you pray. You might feel a little strange or uncomfortable with the silence, but I want to ask you to give it a try to see what happens. God can surprise us sometimes and show up in ways we don't normally expect."

Sometimes it's helpful to talk about the different ways we're in relationship with other people: we talk, we listen, we do things together, and sometimes we're just together, without words. Try to help youth see that the prayer is similar to listening or just being with a friend without speaking.

Be sure to acknowledge difficulties. Point out what may not work. Make sure kids understand there is no "right" way to experience the exercise. I often say something like, "Sometimes when we pray it's difficult to focus—our minds are moving too fast, we're tired, or maybe this just isn't the best way for us to pray. That's okay. Don't get stressed if you're having a hard time with this exercise. Just simply say within yourself, 'God, I want to be with you right now,' and let everything else fall away."

Allow the group to get physically comfortable before you start.

## PRAYER

Lead group members in a centering exercise as you begin the prayer. Darken the room and light a candle to help them focus their attention. Have them pay attention to their breath, relax their body, and turn their attention toward God. You may prefer to have the group sing a simple chorus to help prepare their hearts for prayer.

Invite the youth to dedicate the time to God. Remind them that their desire to be with God is what's most important in prayer. Then simply allow the group to spend some time in prayer. Make sure you pray along with the youth. Trust that God is at work—try to ease up on monitoring the kids. If there are kids who become disruptive, speak the truth in love. Call them back to prayer using an economy of words. In silence we often worry that nothing is "happening." Remember that silence is God's first language—try to let go of worries about whether or not the exercise is "working."

At the end of the prayer time, invite youth to offer thanks to God for whatever occurred during prayer. Have an appropriate closing for the prayer (maybe the Lord's Prayer or a simple song) and then make the transition back to the group.

contemplative youth ministry

## TESTIMONY

Sometimes at the close of the prayer it might be appropriate to invite the youth to express their prayer experience through some physical act or ritual: lighting a candle, placing a rock before a cross, etc. Other times it might be important to have kids spend time journaling their experiences. Even after journaling it's helpful to invite youth to speak their experience in the larger group. It's good for kids to hear the variety of experiences within prayer. This also gives the leaders a chance to answer questions and respond to theological or spiritual issues that arise.

If you give kids a chance to talk about their experience, make sure you respond with open-hearted, nonjudgmental remarks. You don't know what God is doing within these young people, so be open. If you're concerned about a young person's prayer experience, follow up with that youth privately. Let kids know that this exercise may not work for everyone—it's just an exercise; it's not God. Allow people to talk about "flat" experiences as well: "I fell asleep." "I couldn't focus." "I had no sense that God was present in this prayer." Such experiences are common for both youth and adults.

Let kids know that their prayer experience, whether enlightening or flat, is all part of trying to be in relationship with God and is common among Christians throughout history. Remind them again that their desire to be with God is what's most important and pleasing to God.

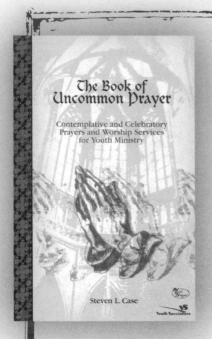

Written in a language your students can understand, this collection of services, prayers, devotions, and readings are ideal for any occasion. Regardless of denomination, you'll find prayers for Christmas, final exams, family, loving enemies, and more. Includes the music CD, *Eucharist*, with worship songs from the U.K.

**The Book of Uncommon Prayer 1**
Contemplative and Celebratory Prayers and Worship Services for Youth Ministry
Steven Case
RETAIL $19.99
ISBN 0-310-24142-1

This collection of scripted services, blessings, rites, and prayers meet the growing desire of young people to step away from the noise of their lives and linger in a slower, quieter place. Geared toward all denominations and all levels of ministry involvement, *The Book of Uncommon Prayer 2* will draw your students to the still, quiet love of Christ.

**The Book of Uncommon Prayer 2**
Prayers and Worship Services for Youth Ministry
Steven Case
RETAIL $19.99
ISBN 0-310-26723-4